C000156470

International Tank Developments From 1970

Alexander Lüdeke

Translated by Geoffrey Brookes

Pen & Sword
MILITARY

Originally published as *Kampfpanzer: Internationale Entwicklungen seit 1970*
Copyright © 2013, Motorbuch Verlag, Stuttgart

First published in Great Britain in 2018 by
Pen & Sword Military
an imprint of
Pen & Sword Books Ltd
47 Church Street
Barnsley
South Yorkshire
S70 2AS

Copyright © Alexander Lüdeke 2018

ISBN 978 1 47389 141 8

Typeset in Ehrhardt by
Mac Style Ltd, Bridlington, East Yorkshire
Printed and bound in India by Replika Press Pvt. Ltd

Pen & Sword Books Ltd incorporates the imprints of Pen & Sword Archaeology, Atlas, Aviation, Battleground, Discovery, Family History, History, Maritime, Military, Naval, Politics, Railways, Select, Transport, True Crime, and Fiction, Frontline Books, Leo Cooper, Praetorian Press, Seaforth Publishing and Wharncliffe.

For a complete list of Pen & Sword titles please contact
PEN & SWORD BOOKS LIMITED
47 Church Street, Barnsley, South Yorkshire, S70 2AS, England
E-mail: enquiries@pen-and-sword.co.uk
Website: www.pen-and-sword.co.uk

Contents

The 1970s marked a turning point in tank building with the advent of new technologies revolutionizing design, construction and battlefield deployment. Compound and explosive reactive armour (ERA) made a degree of protection possible which had been inconceivable previously.

Compound- or layered armour in a simple form appeared for the first time in the mid-1960s fitted to the Soviet T-64. Also effective in the same era was *Chobham* armour developed in Great Britain. The exact composition of modern compound armour remains classified, but in principle consists of ceramic tiles (e.g. boron carbide, silicon carbide or aluminium oxide) between steel layers, often combined with other synthetic materials and heavy metals. An arrangement of several layers of steel of differing temper one behind the other with rubber layers inbetween also contributes to the protection. Thus the turret front of the 2A5 *Leopard* has a resistance equivalent to about 900 mm (c. 35 inches) armoured

steel against KE shells. Against HEAT (high explosive hollow charge anti-tank) ammunition this resistance is of the order of 1700 mm.

ERA was first used in combat by the Israelis in the Lebanon War of 1982 and was their response to the massive losses suffered under hollow-charge fire during the Yom Kippur War of 1973. ERA was not an Israeli invention, however: the first trials had been carried out by the Soviets shortly after the Second World War, and research was also in hand at the end of the 1960s in Germany. ERA, a thin layer of explosive covered by a steel plate, is used mostly as outer slabs or tiles. A shell hitting this "tiling" ignites the explosive which then fires the steel plate against it. The system is very effective against a hollow-charge shell, reducing its penetrating force considerably. It is much less effective against KE shells, and a disadvantage is that it can present some danger to supporting infantry.

As a reaction to the introduction of compound and ERA, new APFSDS anti-tank ammunition was

The Finnish Army possessed around 160 T-72M1, some of which had seen service previously with the Czech Peoples Army. (Finnish Forces)

developed which overcame to some extent the new technology, but nevertheless modern battle tanks have a substantially better level of protection than their predecessors.

Since the 1970s work has proceeded on defensive systems aimed at bestowing invulnerability upon a tank, these systems being known as Soft-Kill and Hard-Kill. The former disrupts the guidance system of anti-tank missiles and is often coupled to anti-laser warning equipment which releases smoke upon detecting that the tank has been picked out by a laser aiming device. The Hard-Kill detects incoming projectiles by radar, calculates the time and coordinates of impact by computer and takes action mainly by a "charge of small-shot". Although successful against anti-tank missiles in trials, the proof of efficiency against APFSDS ammunition remains to be determined.

There are also major improvements in the areas of targeting devices, sensors and fire control. The introduction of computer based fire-control installations (which also take into account air pressure, wind direction and windspeed), laser rangefinders and new, stabilized optics increase the first-round-hit probability considerably (even when on the move). Residual light (low light level enhancers) and thermal imagery are much more effective than infra-red searchlights for identifying targets at night. The heat given off by an object can also be used to very good effect during periods of poor visibility.

All these innovations proved successful during the operations *Desert Storm* in 1991 and *Iraqi Freedom* in 2003 and resulted in a towering superiority over the Iraqi tanks, which were mostly old and of Soviet and Chinese origin. Nevertheless, these easy victories should not be overvalued, for in the main, the equipment of the Iraqis in 1991 was obsolete. Their tank ammunition dated from the early 1970s while training of the crews left much to be desired.

Modern battle tanks have a comprehensive computer installation including a navigation and battlefield management system which represents the tactical situation on a screen. Furthermore a tank can be linked into a network with companion vehicles. Such inclusion into military computer networks is becoming increasingly more important.

Tank battles such as were seen in the Yom Kippur War or during Operation *Desert Storm* in 1991 do not seem likely in future, at least not for the ground forces of the Western armies, following the end of the Cold War and the collapse of the Soviet Union in 1991. The massive inventory of NATO tanks has been reduced annually since the beginning of the 1990s, and new developments have practically come to a stop. Nowadays peacekeeping or suppressive measures, the so-called asymmetric warfare against insurgency and terrorism, have come to the forefront. In these circumstances the battle tank has to operate in areas long considered unsuitable for successful deployment: well developed, densely occupied territory. The Russians learned the hard way that cities are anything but suitable for armour alone when their forces lost many tanks destroyed during the attack on Grozny, capital of Chechen. For success in the urban environment close cooperation is required with supporting infantry, as well as appropriate equipment. For this reason specialized gear for this kind of operation has recently been offered, e.g. TUSK (Tank Urban Survival Kit) for the A1 *Abrams* or the *Leopard* 2A7+., while developers are also focussed on providing better protection against landmines and explosive devices.

It is difficult to predict the direction of future development. What is certain is that rising costs for military programmes in the absence of funds from the national treasuries, and the lack of a current enemy, guarantee that the development of completely new battle tanks is unlikely in the forseeable future. The United States is planning to retain at least 2,050 of their M1A2 in service. Exceptions are South Korea and Japan which have an aggressive and unpredictable neighbour in North Korea. Therefore both continue now as before with large fleets of tanks and are currently in the process of introducing two ultra-modern models in the K2 and Type 10.

The enormous weight of modern battle tanks in excess of 60 tonnes causes logistical problems.

Transport by air is only seldom feasible and many bridges cannot bear this kind of weight. This might mean that future battle tanks will be lighter, and fitted with modular armour adequate for the degree of threat of the times. By using modern materials and new techniques such as NERA (non-explosive reactive armour) or protective systems designed to intercept incoming projectiles at a distance, designers will no doubt attempt to maintain the degree of protection or improve it. For the present the battle tank retains its place on the battlefield and is now as before the central component of the land forces of many nations.

Acknowledgements

Numerous institutions, firms and private persons assisted in the production of this book under the Typenkompass imprint. My thanks go to them all. I would like to make special mention of Vincent Bourguignon, Massimo Foti, Alf von Beem, Vitaly V. Kuzmin, Paul Appleyard, Simon Quinton, Zachi Evinor and Lawrence Skuse. My thanks also go to my life-partner Martina Pohl and our son Thore without whose patience and support this work would not have been possible.

Glossary

APFSDS	Armour-piercing fin-stabilized discarding sabot
APU	Auxiliary power unit
Bundeswehr	(West-) German Federal Army
ERA	Explosive reactive armour
GLONASS	Russian global satellite navigation system (counterpart to GPS)
HEAT	High explosive anti-tank (hollow charge ammunition)
HESH	High explosive squash head (ammunition)
HL	Hollow charge
IR	Infra-red
KE	Kinetic energy
L/xx	Length of cannon barrel expressed in relationship to the calibre: therefore a 120-mm cannon L/50 has a barrel 6 metres long (120-mmx50=600 mm)
NBC	Anti-nuclear, biological, chemical installation
NERA	Non-explosive reactive armour
Schott	A term with no equivalent in English, the German word means "bulkhead". It is armour composed of several kinds of steel plates in layers, the outer plate being of high resistance, the inner of high ductility.
TUSK	Tank Urban Survival Kit
Vielstoff	Motor able to run on diesel, benzine, kerosene or other mixture of fuels.

A Norwegian Leopard 2A4 in snow. (Norwegian Forces)

Ramses II

At the end of 1984, Teledyne Continental Motors (TCM, nowadays General Dynamics Land Systems) received from the Egyptian Army a contract to upgrade the firepower and mobility of one of their T-54s. This prototype was designated initially as T-54E (E for Egypt), but later named *Ramses II* (after the Pharoah of the same name). This modernized T-54 arrived in Egypt at the beginning of 1987 where it underwent extensive trials, and it was planned that the model would enter service in 2004 after another 425 T-54s and T-55s had been modernized in Egypt. Apparently the programme was stopped after about 260 tanks had been converted. The most striking feature in comparison to the T-54/55 is the longer hull which now has six rolling wheels (the same as on the M-48), new hydropneumatic suspension and new tracks. The new motor, a TCM 908-hp diesel, has RENK automatic transmission. Main armament is a 105-mm M68 retaining the recoil system and breech ring of the old 100-mm cannon. A digital fire-control installation, new sights, a laser rangefinder and

thermal imaging equipment have improved accuracy. Together with other minor improvements, the *Ramses II* is a major improvement on the T-54/55.

The original prototype T-54E on trials in the United States. The series vehicles have additional lateral aprons covering the tracks and reactive additional armour is optional. (General Dynamics Land Systems)

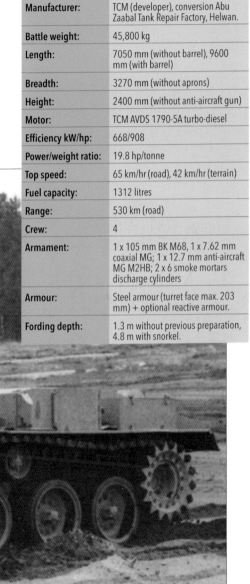

Type:	Ramses II
Manufacturer:	TCM (developer), conversion Abu Zaabal Tank Repair Factory, Helwan.
Battle weight:	45,800 kg
Length:	7050 mm (without barrel), 9600 mm (with barrel)
Breadth:	3270 mm (without aprons)
Height:	2400 mm (without anti-aircraft gun)
Motor:	TCM AVDS 1790-5A turbo-diesel
Efficiency kW/hp:	668/908
Power/weight ratio:	19.8 hp/tonne
Top speed:	65 km/hr (road), 42 km/hr (terrain)
Fuel capacity:	1312 litres
Range:	530 km (road)
Crew:	4
Armament:	1 x 105 mm BK M68, 1 x 7.62 mm coaxial MG; 1 x 12.7 mm anti-aircraft MG M2HB; 2 x 6 smoke mortars discharge cylinders
Armour:	Steel armour (turret face max. 203 mm) + optional reactive armour.
Fording depth:	1.3 m without previous preparation, 4.8 m with snorkel.

TAM (Tanque Argentino Mediano – Argentine Medium Tank)

Because its own industry had no experience in building armoured vehicles, in 1974 the Argentine Government gave Thyssen-Henschel a contract to develop a medium tank to be produced in Argentina. In cooperation with Argentine engineers, the German firm designed and built three TAM prototypes by 1977 based on the *Marder* 1 infantry fighting vehicle. Besides designing the TAM battle tank, the development of an armoured personnel-carrier (*vehículo de combate transporte de personal* or VCTP, also based on the *Marder*) was also included in the contract. Production in Argentina began in 1979 but was halted in 1983 due to financial problems after 150 TAM had been completed. After Peru cancelled a contract in 1983, the Argentine Army received another 20 TAM earmarked for export. Production in Argentina was resumed in 1994 but concluded finally

Type:	TAM
Manufacturer:	TAMSE
Battle weight:	30,500 kg
Length:	6243 mm (without barrel), 8859 mm (with barrel)
Breadth:	3270 mm (without track aprons)
Height:	2807 mm (with AA gun)
Motor:	12150L-7BW V-12 diesel
Efficiency kW/hp:	427/580
Power/weight ratio:	15.8 hp/tonne
Top speed:	50 km/hr (road), 25 km/hr (terrain)
Fuel capacity:	935 litres (internal) 2 x 200 litre additional tanks at rear (optional)
Range:	440 km without, or 600 km with, additional tanks
Crew:	4
Armament:	1 x 100-mm BK 1 x 7.62-mm Type 59T coaxial MG 1 x 12.7-mm AA MG Type 54
Armour:	Steel armour (20-203 mm)
Fording depth:	1.4 m without previous preparation, 4.8 m with snorkel

This photograph of an early TAM clearly shows its affinity to the Marder *armoured personnel-carrier.*

A TAM of the Argentine Army seen in May 2008 in Buenos Aires. Notice the snorkel protruding from the command cupola used for fording at depth. (Joaquín Alvarez Riera)

the following year after 236 TAM had been turned out. The assembly line was then shut down. Around 70% of the TAM components were manufactured in Argentina, the remainder (including transmission, optics and fire-control installation) were imported from West Germany. Although interest in the TAM was expressed by numerous States, the tank was never exported. During the Iran-Iraq War (1980-1988) for example, both sides wanted to obtain hundreds of TAM battle tanks, but the sale was vetoed by the West German Government under political pressure from the United States. The TAM uses the *Marder* hull form and wheel base combined with a more powerful engine and stronger armour offering protection against shells up to 40 mm calibre. Argentina came down firmly in favour of a relatively lighter armour in order to keep the vehicle weight within reasonable limits for the country's streets and bridges. The engine and automatic drive are located right side

forward, the driver sits on the left. The revolving turret towards the rear is fitted with a 105-mm rifled FM K.4 Mod 1L barrel without thermal sleeve, a version of the British L7 licensed for production in Argentina, for which 50 rounds are carried.

Together with the VCTP based on the TAM there are also a 155-mm armoured howitzer (VCA 155), a mortar carrier (VCPM) and a command vehicle (VCPC). Other variants failed to proceed beyond the prototype stage.

There are future plans for the TAM to be modernized by Elbit Systems (Israel). This work will include a new electrical turret pivot drive, new night vision equipment, a linked-in tactical battle management system, a thermal protection sleeve for the cannon, a laser warning system, a new fire extinguisher installation and an auxiliary power unit (APU). Possibly a new 120-mm cannon will be installed as well.

Type 69

The development of Type 69 (WZ-121) had already begun by 1963 when it was held back in the confusion of the Cultural Revolution. Not until the Chinese succeeded in capturing a T-62 in 1969 during the border incidents on the Ussuri was the development resumed. The Chinese decided to include some features of the T-62, amongst them the fully stabilized smooth bore cannon and infra-red searchlight. The 115-mm cannon was copied but in a smaller 100-mm version, thus avoiding the comprehensive alterations to hull and turret which had been necessary for the T-62 when replacing the T-54/55 series.

In comparison to the Type 59 the armour at the front of the hull was increased slightly and a 580-hp diesel fitted. The Type 69-I had an improved IR searchlight and an NBC system. Neither version met the expectations of the Peoples Liberation Army (PLA), especially not the smooth bore cannon and fire control system, and were rejected. In 1982 the much improved Type 69-II appeared with a new fire-control installation, laser-rangefinder above the cannon, and a fully stabilized 100-mm rifled barrel. Later Type 69-II's had a wire grille around the sides and rear of the turret as protection against hollow-charge shells, and track aprons. Although the PLA ordered only a few Type 69s, the Type was exported in large

Type:	Type 69-II
Manufacturer:	NORINCO
Battle weight:	36,700 kg
Length:	6243 mm (without barrel), 8859 mm (with barrel)
Breadth:	3270 mm (without track aprons)
Height:	2807 mm (with AA gun)
Motor:	12150L-7BW V-12 diesel
Efficiency kW/hp:	427/580
Power/weight ratio:	15.8 hp/tonne
Top speed:	50 km/hr (road), 25 km/hr (terrain)
Fuel capacity:	935 litres (internal) 2 x 200 litre additional tanks at rear (optional)
Range:	440 km without, or 600 km with, additional tanks
Crew:	4
Armament:	1 x 100-mm BK 1 x 7.62-mm Type 59T coaxial MG 1 x 12.7-mm AA MG Type 54
Armour:	Steel armour (20-203 mm)
Fording depth:	1.4 m without previous preparation, 4.8 m with snorkel

numbers. During the 1980s around 2,000 Type 69s went for export, the major client being Iraq which took over a thousand of them. Variants 69-IIB and C

US Marines looking over a captured Iraqi Type 69-II during Operation Desert Storm at the beginning of 1991. The Type 69 is a further development of Type 59 and outwardly almost indistinguishable from it. (USMC)

An Iraqi Type 69-II captured by French forces in 1991. Notice the laser rangefinder on the cannon and the infra-red searchlight to the right of the barrel and in front of the commander's cupola. (Massimo Foti, Saumur Tank Museum, 27.10.2010)

are command vehicles with additional radio and communications equipment.

The Type 69-II was also built under licence in Pakistan and given local modifications in service by users such as Iraq and Bangladesh. The Iraqi Type 69-QM is a Type 69-II with additional *schott* armour at the front of the hull. Some command vehicles were given passive additional armour to the turret and hull sides. The QM-1 was fitted with a 105-mm cannon with rifled barrel and laser- rangefinder, while the QM-2 (apparently only prototypes) received the 125-mm smooth bore 2A46 cannon and T-72M1 automatic loading carousel magazine. Bangladesh equipped some of its Type 69-II's with the 105-mm cannon with rifled barrel, new tracks and reactive armour. The Type 69-IIG (*Gai*) has a 120-mm smooth bore cannon able to fire missiles. It has a semi-automatic loading system, a 1000-hp diesel, explosive reactive armour and passive additional armour, a new digital fire control system with integrated laser-rangefinder and thermal imaging, and a GPS.

The Type 69 has two searchlights on the left and right track covers while the only searchlight on the Type 59 (as a rule) is fitted at the front of the hull. (USMC)

Type 79

The Type 79 is a further development of Type 69 with Western components. Therefore the Type 79 has a Chinese version (Type 83) of the British 105-mm rifled cannon barrel with thermal sleeve and a digital fire-control system with a Marconi (British) integral laser-rangefinder. The tank is equipped additionally with passive night vision devices and a 730-hp diesel. The first prototype of this tank, initially known as the type 69-III (WZ-121D), was completed in 1981.

For the first time in Chinese tank building the Type 79 has tracks with rubber padding and NBC protection which automatically closes the hatches upon detecting a threat. The production of Type 79 began in 1984, but only 700 to 800 have been built since. Although apparently built primarily for export, there was some hindrance to offering it on the international market. In Chinese service some of this type were subsequently given a reactive additional armour.

Type:	Type 79
Manufacturer:	NORINCO
Battle weight:	37,500 kg
Length:	6243 mm (without barrel)
Breadth:	3270 mm (without track aprons)
Height:	2807 mm (with AA MG)
Motor:	Model VR-36 V-12 diesel
Efficiency kW/hp:	537/730
Power/weight ratio:	19.47 hp/tonne
Top speed:	50 km/hr (road), 25 km/hr (terrain)
Fuel capacity:	not known
Range:	400 km without, 600 km with, 2 x 200 litre additional tanks at rear
Crew:	4
Armament:	1 x 105-mm Type 83 cannon 1 x 7.62-mm Type 59T coaxial MG 1 x 12.7-mm AA MG Type 54
Armour:	Steel armour (20-203 mm)
Fording depth:	1.4 m without previous preparation, 4.8 m with snorkel

The Type 79 is a further development of the Type 69 and is equipped with a range of Western components.

Type 88

The Type 88 was developed from the beginning of the 1980s and is a derivative of the Type series 59/69/79. The Type 88 has a new, welded hull and new wheelbase design with six small rolling wheels on torsion bars (apparently influenced by the M48 obtained from Vietnam). The turret is in moulded form as previously and very reminiscent of its predecessor. The 730-hp diesel is of German design, the fire-control and stabilizing systems for the main weapon and cannon are British. The first prototype carried the designation "Type 80" and was introduced in 1985. The laser-rangefinder was still fitted at this time above the cannon. A wire grille was fitted at the turret rear. The prototype was redesignated Type 80-II after being fitted with a laser-rangefinder integrated into the gunsight, all situated on the turret roof, new NBC protection and now had a wire grille surrounding the turret for additional protection against HL projectiles.

Type:	Type 88B
Manufacturer:	NORINCO
Battle weight:	39,500 kg
Length:	6325 mm (without barrel), 9328 mm (with barrel)
Breadth:	3372 mm
Height:	2290 mm, 2874 mm (with AA MG)
Motor:	Model VR-36 V-12 turbo-diesel
Efficiency kW/hp:	537/730
Power/weight ratio:	18.48 hp/tonne
Top speed:	60 km/hr (road)
Fuel capacity:	1400 litres (internal)
Range:	430 km without, 600 km with, additional tanks at the rear
Crew:	4
Armament:	1 x 105-mm cannon 1 x 7.62-mm Type 59T coaxial MG 1 x 12.7-mm AA MG Type 54
Armour:	Steel armour (thickness not known)
Fording depth:	1.4 m without previous preparation, 4.8 m with snorkel

The Type 88A has a longer and more efficient 105-mm cannon. (VBA)

Type 88B's of the Peoples Liberation Army, photographs taken during a parade on the Chinese National Day (1 October) in Beijing.

The series production is designated "Type 88" for being introduced in 1988: it has a wire grille only at the rear of the turret. The variant 88B has an improved, computerized fire-control system and modifications to the breech and cannon baseplate. Despite the designation, variant 88A was introduced after version 88B. It is fitted with a more efficient 105-mm cannon Type 83-I with longer barrel. The PLA had 400 to 500 Type 88 tanks manufactured up to 1995, and about the same number were exported to the Sudan, Myanmar (former Burma) and Bangladesh.

Type 85

The Type 85 is based on the undercarriage and chassis of the 80/88 series but the new turret is welded and has compound armour. The first prototype (Type 85) was displayed in 1988 with a 105-mm rifled-barrel cannon. The Type 85-I had a thermal barrel sleeve fitted. The Type 85 was then withheld by the PLA for improvements. The earlier Iraqi T-72, obtained from Iran at the end of the 1980s, influenced the design of the Type 85-II. It has a revolving automatic loader and a new fire-control system. The Type 85-IIA was fitted with a 125-mm smooth bore cannon and exported to Pakistan (around 300 tanks) under the designation Type 85-IIAP. In the mid-1990s the Type 85-IIM came out with better armour and improved fire-control system with passive night vision equipment. The variant 85-III (1996) was equipped with a 1000-hp diesel and ERA tiles on the hull and turret face but did not see service with the PLA. Whereas Pakistan did not require this tank, many of their older Type 85-IIAP's were re-equipped to meet the standard.

Type:	Type 85-IIA
Manufacturer:	NORINCO
Battle weight:	41 tonnes
Length:	10280 mm (with barrel)
Breadth:	3450 mm
Height:	2300 mm (upper side turret)
Motor:	Model VR-36 V-12 turbo-diesel
Efficiency kW/hp:	537/730
Power/weight ratio:	18.48 hp/tonne
Top speed:	60 km/hr (road)
Fuel capacity:	not known
Range:	500 km (from internal fuel tanks)
Crew:	3
Armament:	1 x 125-mm cannon 1 x 7.62-mm Type 59T coaxial MG 1 x 12.7-mm AA MG Type 54 2 x 6 smoke discharge cylinders
Armour:	Steel armour, compound protection
Fording depth:	1.4 m without previous preparation, 4.8 m with snorkel

The Type 85-IIM had features from the T-72 and was introduced in the mid-1990s. The Chinese Peoples Liberation Army has around 600 Type 85s in various versions.

Type 90/MBT-2000

The Type 90, a further development of the Type 85, was exhibited for the first time in 1991. Its front area has a modular compound armour. Apart from a few experimental units the Type 90 was not added to the PLA fleet and was offered instead for export in various forms and designations. During the 1990s amongst others Chinese, German, British, French and Ukraine drive components were tested. Pakistan showed especial interest in this tank and was involved to some extent in its development and also testing. The Type 90-IIM version with 6TD-2 diesel (1200 hp) from the Ukraine suited Pakistani requirements best and since 2001 has been built there under licence with modifications as *Al-Khalid*. In 2001 NORINCO introduced its export version "MBT 2000" of which Bangladesh bought 44 in 2011 for delivery from 2012. Since 2007 NORINCO has also offered the "VT-1A", a modernized version with new turret, improved armour, a more efficient cannon and a Chinese 1300- to 1500-hp diesel. Peru intended to buy a number of these tanks in 2009 but cancelled the order the following year.

Type:	Type 90/MBT-2000
Manufacturer:	NORINCO
Battle weight:	46 tonnes
Length:	10067 mm (with barrel)
Breadth:	3500 mm
Height:	2400 mm (upper side, turret)
Motor:	GTD-2 opposed piston diesel
Efficiency kW/hp:	883/1200
Power/weight ratio:	26.06 hp/tonne
Top speed:	70 km/hr (road)
Fuel capacity:	not known
Range:	500 km (internal tanks)
Crew:	3
Armament:	1 x 125-mm cannon 1 x 7.62-mm coaxial MG 1 x 12.7-mm AA MG 2 x 6 smoke mortars
Armour:	Steel armour, compound protection, ERA optional
Fording depth:	1.4 m without previous preparation, 5 m with snorkel

The MBT 2000 pictured here is the export version of the Type 90. Note the ERA tiles on the turret and at the front of the hull. (NORINCO)

Type 96

The Type 96, built since 1997 (also ZTZ 96 and initially Type 88C) is basically a slightly modified Type 85-III benefiting from experience gained from trials of the Type 90. Like the Type 85, Type 96 is based on results from testing some of the former Iraqi-72 tanks captured by Iran. Thus the hull, the 125-mm cannon and the rotating automatic loader all have Russian hallmarks. On the other hand the cornered welded turret has its origins in Western designs. Hull and turret front protection is partly modular compound armour. The turret sides and rear are surrounded by a stowage grille which also offers additional protection against incoming HL fire. As on the Type 85 predecessor, there are six rollers and three drive wheels, and torsion bar suspension. Motor and gearing are located at the rear of the hull, operationally tracks and suspension are protected by lateral aprons.

Type:	Type 96
Manufacturer:	NORINCO
Battle weight:	42,800 kg
Length:	10280 mm (with barrel)
Breadth:	3450 mm
Height:	2300mm (upper side, turret)
Motor:	Turbo-diesel
Efficiency kW/hp:	735/1000
Power/weight ratio:	23.36 hp/tonne
Top speed:	70 km/hr (road)
Fuel capacity:	not known
Range:	400 km (with internal tanks)
Crew:	3
Armament:	1 x 125-mm cannon 1 x 7.62-mm coaxial MG 1 x 12.7-mm AA MG 2 x 6 smoke mortars
Armour:	Steel armour, compound protection, ERA optional
Fording depth:	1.4 m without previous preparation, 5 m with snorkel

A Type 96 in snow. It is presently the most important main battle tank of the PLA.

Side profile of the Type 96. Note the wire grille on the turret sides and rear which serve as additional protection against incoming HL fire.

Since 2006 an improved version of the Type 96 (Type 96G or also 96A) has been operational. The turret front has wedge-shaped additional armour and the vehicle front is layered with ERA tiles. (All three photos PLA.)

Type 98

At the beginning of the 1970s, China began the development of a tank intended to match modern Western models. A multitude of problems prevented useful prototypes from being completed before 1991. The hull and armament was strongly influenced by the T-72 while the turrets resembled Western designs. Before the pre-series vehicles were approved in 1998 the model had been tested for years and subjected to repeated modifications. The driver is seated in the centre forward, the two-man turret is fitted with a 125-mm cannon and self-loader, the diesel motor and transmission are at the rear. The Type 98 (also ZTZ-98) has modular compound armour with ERA as an optional extra. A modern digital fire-control system with laser rangefinder, heat imager and crosswind sensor provide a high degree of accuracy. The Type 98 also has a GPS and GLONASS navigational system. Besides conventional ammunition, AT-11 *Sniper* (9M119) missiles can be fired. A laser warning device fires the smoke mortars automatically if danger is detected. A JD-3 rotatable radar-jamming device is located on the turret roof.

Type:	Type 98
Manufacturer:	NORINCO
Battle weight:	52 tonnes
Length:	11 metres (with barrel)
Breadth:	3400 mm
Height:	2100 (upper side, turret)
Motor:	12-cylinder turbo-diesel
Efficiency kW/hp:	883/1200
Power/weight ratio:	23.1 hp/tonne
Top speed:	70 km/hr (road)
Fuel capacity:	not known
Range:	450 km (internal tanks), 600 km with additional tanks
Crew:	3
Armament:	1 x 125-mm cannon 1 x 7.62-mm coaxial Type 86 MG 1 x 12.7-mm AA Type 85 MG 2 x 5 smoke mortars
Armour:	Steel armour, compound protection, ERA optional
Fording depth:	1.4 m without previous preparation, 5 m with snorkel

A Type 98 on the move. Notice the characteristic diagonal ribbing at the front of the hull. In contrast to the Type 96, the Type 98 still has only five smoke mortars on each side of the turret.

A Type 98 on manoeuvres. (PLA)

Type 98s on parade on China's National Day. Beijing, 1 October 2005. (US DoD)

It would appear that in all only around 120 Type 98s have been completed. Apparently the type was never intended for mass production but served as the pre-series model for the Type 99.

Type 99

The Type 99 (also designated ZTZ-99 or WZ-123) is at present the most modern and efficient battle tank of the PLA. It is a further development of the Type 98 and was introduced in 2001 initially as a Type 98G. In common with its fore-runner the Type 99 has a 125-mm smooth bore cannon loaded automatically from a carousel magazine. It also has the capability to fire AT-11 *Sniper* missiles. The APFSDS round has a muzzle velocity of 1780 m/sec and according to Chinese reports the tungsten-capped shell can go through 850 mm steel armour, and the uranium-capped shell through 960 mm steel armour at a range of 2000 metres. The fire-control installation, optics and electronic equipment appear to correspond to those of the Type 98. A JD-3 radar-jamming device is located on the turret roof and can allegedly "blind" a laser-guided missile, and presumably also damage enemy optics and the eyes of the operators. The most striking difference from the earlier version is the wedge-shaped additional protection at the turret front, which can be strengthened by the addition of reactive armour. The

Type:	Type 99A1
Manufacturer:	NORINCO
Battle weight:	57 tonnes
Length:	11 metres (with barrel)
Breadth:	3400 mm
Height:	2200 mm (upper side, turret)
Motor:	150 HB 12-cylinder turbo diesel
Efficiency kW/hp:	1103/1500
Power/weight ratio:	26.3 hp/tonne
Top speed:	80 km/hr (road), 60 km/hr (terrain)
Fuel capacity:	not known
Range:	450 km (with internal tanks), 600 km with additional tanks
Crew:	3
Armament:	1 x 125-mm cannon 1 x 7.62-mm coaxial Type 86 MG 1 x 12.7-mm AA Type 85 MG 2 x 5 smoke mortars
Armour:	Steel armour, compound protection, ERA
Fording depth:	1.4 m without previous preparation, 5 m with snorkel

The Type 99 is presently the most up-to-date Chinese battle tank. (PLA)

A Type 99 tank on manouevres. Note the ERA blocks on the hull and turret fronts, and the turret sides. (PLA)

front of the hull and the rear of the turret are also cloaked with ERA tiles.

The Type 99 was equipped additionally with a 1500-hp diesel, said to be based on the German MTU MB 873 found aboard the *Leopard*. Many details about the Type 99 and its variants remain unclear. It is known that since 2001 a number of variants have emerged, but whether these are from a series or only experimental vehicles remains uncertain. The literature has the original version Type 99 (or 98G), the version A1 (in two variants, distinguished by the shape of the turret roof), and the newest model with the (probable) designation A2 (but perhaps also Type 99G). The A2 was under test as from 2007 and has a modified armour for the turret front, new optics for the tank commander, and a different electro-optic jamming device now located higher up. There is some controversy as to whether there is a *Hard-Kill* system with millimetre-frequency radar to go with the mentioned *Soft-Kill* devices. The ERA blocks on the turret sides seem much larger, as do the lateral aprons. In contrast to the Type 96, which makes up the bulk of the PLA's modern tanks, by reason of its higher cost of manufacture the Type 99 will only find its place in elite units. Only a few hundred were to have been built by 2012.

This photograph, apparently computer-modified, shows one of the possible configurations of the Type 99A2.

Leopard 2 (A0-A4)

Following the termination of the US-West German project *Kampfpanzer 70*, the firms of Krauss-Maffei, Wegmann and Porsche were assigned the task in 1970 of building a new battle tank alone. The starting point was the experimental development *Keiler* begun two years before. The new design was given the name *Leopard 2* in 1971, and the first prototypes were completed in 1972. As the result of what had been learnt from the Yom Kippur War (1973), it was realized that the armour needed to be upgraded. The conversion now looked more square and was heavier at well over 50 tonnes. At trials in the United States in 1976 comparing the *Leopard 2* with the XM1, both sides found the American tank the better of the two. For the US, both models matched up in firepower and mobility but the XM1 armour was superior. The first *Leopard 2* series reached the units in October 1979.

The hull and rotating turret are welded and both have a combination of compound and *Schottpanzerung* very effective against HL and KE projectiles. The driver sits forward on the right side in the hull near an ammunition bunker. Motor and

Type:	Leopard 2A4
Manufacturer:	Krauss-Maffei (today KMW), MaK (today Rheinmetall Landsysteme)
Battle weight:	55,150 kg
Length:	7722 mm (hull) 9668 mm (with barrel)
Breadth:	3750 mm (with track aprons)
Height:	2480 mm (upper edhe turret), 2990 mm (overall)
Motor:	MB 873-Ka501 Vielstoff (see Glossary) 12-cylinder
Efficiency kW/hp:	1103/1500
Power/weight ratio:	29.3 hp/tonne
Top speed:	72 km/hr (road)
Fuel capacity:	1160 litres
Range:	500 km
Crew:	4
Armament:	1 x 120mm cannon L/44 1 x 7.62 mm coaxial MG 1 x 7.62 mm air defence MG 2 x 8 smoke mortars
Armour:	Steel armour and compound protection
Fording depth:	1.20 m, 4 m with snorkel

A Leopard 2A4 of the Bundeswehr. (KMW)

The Leopard 2A4 is used by numerous European States and worldwide. Seen here is a Leopard 2 of the Finnish Army which from 2002 received 139 Leopard 2A4 from the German inventory, of which 112 were put to use as battle tanks. (Finnish Forces)

A Leopard 2A4 of the Austrian Federal Army firing live rounds at the Allentsteig troop training depot. From 1996 Austria procured a total of 114 Leopard 2A4s which had previously seen service in the Netherlands Army. In 2006 forty of them were singled out and sold back to the manufacturer KMW in 2011. (Austrian Federal Army)

transmission are located at the rear. The three-man rotating turret at the centre of the tank is fitted with a 120-mm smooth bore cannon Rh 120 L/44 (with smoke extractor and thermal barrel jacket), a coaxial 7.62-mm MG and air defence MG of the same calibre. The sighting optics of the *Leopard 2* are fully stabilized, the cannon is adjusted hydraulically. Thus even in motion the weapon and optics remain on the target and in combination with a digital fire-control installation and laser-rangefinder provide a high first-round-hit probability. The chassis has seven rolling wheels per side with torsion bar suspension, partially protected by track aprons. Officially the 1500 hp motor gives the tank a top speed of 72 km/hr, but on good roads 100 km/hr has been reached. The first Leopard 2 (AO) models had a crosswind sensor but were not fitted with thermal imaging equipment(WBG). They still had at that time a low-light level camera PZB 200 until the ex-works A1 version with WBG appeared with other improvements but less the crosswind sensor. With all these changes the A1 became the A2. The variant A3 differed only in detail. The major version is the A4 model (end of 1985 to March 1992) which had new track aprons, a field adjusting apparatus, an improved fire-control system, thicker turret armour and other modifications. All earlier versions were upgraded to the A4 standard so that the Bundeswehr eventually had 2125 A4s. Some of this A4 version (a number of them with minor changes) went to the Netherlands (445) and Switzerland (380). After the end of the Cold War the *Leopard* 2A4 (some altered before despatch or modified by the recipient countries) was exported to Austria, Canada, Chile, Denmark, Finland, Greece, Norway, Poland, Portugal, Singapore, Spain, Sweden and Turkey.

Top: Since 2007 Singapore has had 102 Leopard 2A4s. These tanks were fitted out by IBD Deisenroth Engineering with the Evolution-Packet and shown to the public for the first time on Singapore's National Day in 2010. A similar Packet was developed in Turkey but has so far not been introduced by the Turkish Army, equipped with 354 used A4s.

Bottom: A Leopard 2A4 of the Austrian Federal Army on manouevres. (Österreichisches Bundesheer)

Leopard 2 (A5-A7+)

The Leopard 2A5 version emerged between 1995 and 2002 from the conversion of tanks at hand (350 Bundeswehr, 330 Dutch) and has as its most striking feature a wedge-shaped additional armour at the turret front and new track guards with a straight lower edge. The A5 also has a new design of commander's periscope with its own thermal imagining, an electrical gunlaying and stabilization system, a rear-view camera, an inertial navigation system with GPS, it can take the 120-mm L/55 cannon and has other minor changes.

The A6 version (Bundeswehr 225, Netherlands 180) is similar to the A5 but has the 120-mm L/55 cannon fitted providing higher muzzle velocity. This weapon fires newly developed KE ammunition capable of penetrating 1000-mm steel armour (or equivalent). With additional anti-landmine protection the A6 becomes the A6M. The A5 and A6 versions are or were used by the Netherlands, Canada, Portugal, Greece, Sweden and Spain besides Germany itself. One of the most modern variants is the *Leopard* 2 PSO or A7+ modified especially for operations in built-up areas. Its equipment is completely modular

Type:	Leopard 2A6
Manufacturer:	Krauss-Maffei (today KMW), MaK (today Rheinmetall Landsysteme)
Battle weight:	59,900 kg (A6M 62,500 kg)
Length:	7722 mm (hull) 10970 mm (with barrel)
Breadth:	3750 mm (with track guards)
Height:	2480 mm (upper side turret) 3030 mm overall
Motor:	MB 873-Ka 501 12-cylinder Vielstoff (see Glossary)
Efficiency kW/hp:	1103/1500
Power/weight ratio:	25 hp/tonne
Top speed:	72 km/hr (road)
Fuel capacity:	1160 litres
Range:	500 km
Crew:	4
Armament:	1 x 120mm cannon L/55 1 x 7.62 mm coaxial MG3 1 x 7.62 mm air defence MG3 2 x 8 smoke mortars
Armour:	Steel armour and compound protection
Fording depth:	1.20 m, but 4 m with snorkel

Leopard 2A5 battle tanks of the Bundeswehr on a battle-training exercise at Luttmersen, 17 August 2010. (Bundeswehr/Modes)

Artist's impression of the longer 120-mm L/55 cannon installed on the Leopard 2A6. (Vincent Bourguignon)

A Canadian Leopard 2A6M CAN with wire-grille protection against HL projectiles. The tank is fitted with the Saab Barracuda Mobile Camouflage System (MCS), a kind of camouflage netting which reduces the thermal and radar signature of a vehicle and also shields the interior of the tank against excessive solar heat. Province Kandahar, Afghanistan, 23 December 2010. (US Navy)

and can be adapted for use in all sitautions. Besides additional armoured elements the variant has a remote-controlled weapons and sensor station on the turret, an armoured all-round periscope, tank-infantry phone TIP, a 360° camera system, back-up motor and a mine clearance shield. The Bundeswehr is planning to acquire a certain number of conversion sets from 2019. It became known in the summer of 2012 that

A Leopard 2 PSO (Peace Support Operations) seen here fitted with a mine clearance shield. Munster, 6 September 2010. (Bundeswehr/Trotzki)

Saudi Arabia was intending to buy up to 800 new A7+. Whether this purchase, or the wish of Qatar and Indonesia to have modern Leopard 2s will be approved, remains to be seen.

The *Leopard* 2 was the basis for the pioneer tank *Kodiak*, the armoured recovery tank *Büffel*, a mine clearance vehicle, training vehicle and two bridge-layers.

The *Leopard* 2 has an outstanding reputation worldwide and is considered one of the best – if not the best – battle tank in the world. It provides a balanced combination of mobility, protection and firepower and has set standards in many areas.

Top and bottom: The Leopard 2A7+ developed on private initiative by manufacturer KMW is optimized for operations in urban surroundings. (KMW)

AMX-56 Leclerc

The first planning for the successor to AMX-30 began in 1977, various experimental vehicles being tried out, but it was not until 1989 that the first prototypes of AMX-56 appeared. The first series-built tank came off the line in December 1991 and was issued to the French Army in January 1992. The AMX-56 was the first in Western tank building to have an automatic loader (12 rounds/minute), the ammunition being fed from a 22-round magazine in the rear. 18 other shells are stored on the right-hand side near the driver. The main weapon is a fully stabilized 120-mm smooth bore CN 120-26/52 L/52 with field adjusting apparatus and thermal barrel jacket. The cannon has no smoke extractor, gases are forced out through the

Artist's impression of a Leclerc of 2. Tank Brigade/6.Regt.Cuirassiers, France 2004. (Vincent Bourguignon)

Type:	AMX-56 Leclerc
Manufacturer:	GIAT Industries (today Nexter)
Battle weight:	56,500 kg
Length:	6880 mm (hull), 9870 mm (with barrel)
Breadth:	3710 mm
Height:	2530 mm (upper side turret)
Motor:	SACM V8X 8-cyclinder Hyperbar diesel
Efficiency kW/hp:	1103/1500
Power/weight ratio:	26.55 hp/tonne
Top speed:	72 km/hr (road)
Fuel capacity:	1300 litres (optional 2 x 200 litre external tanks at rear)
Range:	550 km, 650 km with additional tanks
Crew:	3
Armament:	1 x 120-mm CN cannon 120-26/52 L/52 1 x 12.7-mm coaxial MG M2 1 x 7.62 mm air defence MG 2 x 9 smoke mortars
Armour:	Steel and modular compound armour
Fording depth:	1 metre without snorkel

barrel by excess pressure. There is a coaxial 12.7-mm MG. Although the cannon can fire 120-mm Rheinmetall ammunition theoretically, only French ammunition is used in practice. By reason of its relatively short hull, the AMX-56 Leclerc (named after a General of the Free French Forces of the Second World War) has only six running wheels per side, suspension is hydropneumatic. The digital, fully integrated fire-control installation is one of the most modern in the world with laser rangefinder, thermal imagining and low light level amplifier, GPS-based inertial navigation installation and battlefield management system. Another novelty introduced with the AMX-56 is a modular compound armour capable of replacement if battle-damaged, or for modernization. In dangerous situations the GALIX self-protection and smoke mortars integrated into the rear sides of the turret can fire fragmentation-, tear gas-, flare- or IR-disruptive projectiles.

The structure of the *Leclerc* is more compact than other Western tanks, space being saved by having only a three-man crew and a very compact Hyperbar-diesel. The V8X-1500 is a combination of diesel motor and integrated gas turbine, in which the pre-condensed air of the diesel comes from the compressor stage of the turbine, thus avoiding the feared *Turboloch* [turbo drag]. These advantages were

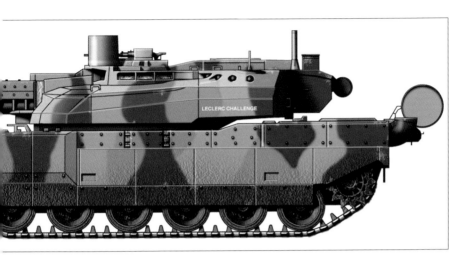

AMX-56 Leclerc of 503.Tank Regt., Paris, 13 July 2006. (RAMA cc by sa 2.0)

obtained at a price, however, by virtue of their complexity and the comparatively high consumption of fuel.

In all, 406 AMX-56 tanks were built in three series for the French Army. The second series (1997-2003) has an improved anti-NBC system with integrated air-conditioning plant, a rear-view camera and other minor modifications. Series 3 (2003-2005) has reinforced armour, a new thermal imaging apparatus, a laser rangefinder within the commander's optic and an improved battlefield management system. The version for the UAE (*Leclerc* EAU) is fitted with a Geman MTU 1500-hp motor which required a lengthening of the hull by 30 cms. In addition this

The Leclerc AZUR is specially equipped for fighting in urban areas and has a remote-controlled weapons plant on the turret, reinforced track aprons and grille protection at the rear. (GIAT)

variant has new track aprons, revised armour and electronics, a new air conditioning unit and a remote-controlled MG on the turret roof. Other variants are two armoured recovery types (*Leclerc* DNG and MARS), a pioneer tank (*Leclerc* EPG) and a training vehicle. A bridgelayer (PTG) was not built in series. The *Leclerc* AZUR, a special version for combat in urban areas, has amongst other features a remote-controlled weapons station on the turret, reinforced track aprons and grille protection at the rear.

Up to 2006, France had supplied herself with 406 battle- and 20 armoured recovery tanks, the UAE had 388 and 46 respectively. In 2011 France had only 254 *Leclerc* battle tanks in service and was hoping to export used tanks to Columbia and Qatar.

An AMX-56 Leclerc in the streets of Paris on Bastille Day, 14 July 2010. (Alf van Beem)

Vickers Main Battle Tank (MBT) Mk III

The Vickers MBT Mk III introduced in 1975 was designed for the export market and had many characteristics of the Mk I. Thus the hull and chassis with six roller wheels on torsion bars is identical, but the turret is much modified with a new cast steel front, and the drive can consist of various diesels in the 700-800 hp range with automatic transmission. The Mk III has a modern fire-control system with laser rangefinder and passive night vision equipment providing the 105-mm rifled barrel L/7 with a high first-round-hit probability. Vickers also designed an armoured recovery- and bridgelayer tank on the basis of the Mk III. The major client was Nigeria which bought 136 fighting tanks, 26 bridgelayers and 12 armoured recovery tanks; Kenya bought 76 battle tanks and 7 armoured recovery vehicles, Tanzania four armoured recovery vehicles. In 1979 Vickers introduced the prototype of the newly designed 43-tonne Mk IV *Valiant* with *Chobham* compound armour, a modern fire-control installation and a 120-mm cannon. The Mk IV failed to convince any overseas buyers however, and the follow-up prototype Mk VII, which combined the turret of the Mk IV on the Leopard 2 hull and motor, was equally unsuccessful.

Type:	Vickers MBT Mk III
Manufacturer:	Vickers Defence Systems
Battle weight:	39,500 kg
Length:	7561 mm (hull) 9788 mm (with barrel)
Breadth:	3168 mm
Height:	2476 mm (upper side turret), 3099 mm (total height)
Motor:	Detroit 12V-71T 12-cyclinder diesel
Efficiency kW/hp:	530/720
Power/weight ratio:	18.22 hp/tonne
Top speed:	60 km/hr (road)
Fuel capacity:	1000 litres
Range:	490 km
Crew:	4
Armament:	1 x 105-mm L/7 cannon 1 x 12.7 mm short-burst/ ranging MG 1 x 7.62-mm coaxial MG, 1 x 7.62 mm AA MG 2 x 6 smoke mortars
Armour:	17 to 80-mm steel armour
Fording depth:	1.1 metres

On the whole the Vickers MBT Mk III was only a modest sucess on the export market. The Mk IIIM version with a new fire-control system and reactive armour developed in the 1990s for Malaysia was never series-produced. (Vickers)

Challenger 1 FV 4030/4

After the breakdown of the Anglo-West German project to develop a new battle tank (MBT 80) in 1977, the British Army looked for a quick short-term solution. They settled for the Shir 2 (FV 4030/3) tank built for Iran. The design designated FV 4030/4 and modified for European operations had the cannon and fire-control installation of a late *Chieftain*, but a 1200 hp diesel with new transmission, and hydropneumatic suspension. Although other Western tanks of that generation were fitted with a 120-mm smooth bore barrel, the British kept to the proven L/11 with rifled barrel since this fired a larger spectrum of ammunition. The hull and turret were redesigned and given the newly developed *Chobham* armour at the front which gave the tank an unmistakable angular shape. The first series vehicles were delivered in April 1983.

By mid-1990, 400 *Challenger 1*s had been built together with 80 armoured recovery vehicles (CR ARRV). Although *Challenger 1* represented a substantial improvement in armour and mobility over the *Chieftain*, its fire-control system was obsolescent.

Type:	Challenger 1 FV 4030/4
Manufacturer:	Vickers Defence Systems
Battle weight:	62 tonnes
Length:	8327 mm (hull), 11560 mm (with barrel)
Breadth:	3518 mm
Height:	2500 mm (upper side turret), 2950 mm (total height)
Motor:	Perkins-Condor 12V 12-cylinder diesel
Efficiency kW/hp:	883/1200
Power/weight ratio:	19.35 hp/tonne
Top speed:	56 km/hr (road)
Fuel capacity:	1592 litres
Range:	450 km
Crew:	4
Armament:	1 x 120-mm L/11 A5 cannon 1 x 7.62-mm coaxial MG, 1 x 7.62 mm AA MG 2 x 5 smoke mortars
Armour:	Steel armour, Chobham compound armour, ERA optional
Fording depth:	1.07 metres: 4.57 m with snorkel

This Challenger 1 "Churchill" of the Bovington Museum collection was photographed at the end of June 2011. (Paul Appleyard)

This became particularly obvious during the Canadian Army Trophy tank gunnery competition in 1987 in which the *Challenger* 1, although specially modified, came off poorly. The reliability of the tank also gave rise to complaint. In 1990/1991 however, when 180 of the Type took part in Operation *Granby*, the British contribution to *Desert Shield* and *Desert Storm*, it proved the best tank. None was lost and its thermal imagining equipment enabled enemy vehicles to be made out in the hours of darkness and in conditions of poor visibility. One *Challenger 1* even succeeded in destroying an Iraqi tank at 4,100 metres range with the first round fired.

Replacement by *Challenger 2* began in mid-1998, and the last *Challenger 1* was paid off by April 2002. From the end of 1999, Jordan received 392 used *Challenger 1*s, renamed *al-Hussein*, and modified, e.g. with new optics, a more modern fire-control system and a 120-mm smooth bore cannon. Jordan also tried out a programme to fit an unmanned turret with a 120-mm cannon (*Falcon Turret*) but this came to nought.

A Challenger 1 near Kuwait City on the Basra-Kuwait motorway. In the background is a British armoured personnel-carrier and the wreck of a garbage truck. Kuwait, February 1991. (US Army)

Side profile of a Challenger 1 at Bovington, England on 30 June/1 July 2012. (Simon Quinton, flickr.com/simononly)

Before operations in the Gulf War of 1990/1991, Challenger 1 was fitted with ERA armour, and passive supplementary armour on the driver's side at the front and at the sides. The tank also had attachments at the rear for two 200-litre additional fuel tanks. Kuwait/Irak, February 1991. (US Army)

Challenger 2 FV 4034

Although no official requisition had been issued for a successor to the Challenger-1, by the mid-1980s development studies had already begun for a new main battle tank. In 1988 Vickers received from the British Ministry of Defence a contract to build nine prototypes with two additional turret configurations in competition with the *Leclerc*, *Leopard 2* and M1A2 builders. As expected after comparison trials in September 1990 the Vickers design proved the best. Up until 2002 the British Army received 386 *Challenger 2*s and 22 training tanks. Whereas *Challenger 2* (CR 2) resembles its predecessor outwardly and also has the same engine and a similar hydro-pneumatic suspension, it is a completely new design and a really powerful fighting vehicle. Nevertheless the British kept the 120-mm rifled barrel cannon with two-part ammunition for the greater range of the latter and were also of the opinion that HESH ammunition (high explosive squash-head) should be retained because of its effectiveness against lightly armoured targets and buildings. The hull and newly designed turret have the new *Dorchester* compound armour with a layer of depleted uranium which makes the CR2 one of the

Type:	Challenger 2 FV 4034
Manufacturer:	Vickers Defence Systems (today BAE Systems)
Battle weight:	62,500 kgs
Length:	8327 mm (hull) 11550 mm (with barrel)
Breadth:	3520 mm (4200 mm with additional armour)
Height:	2490 mm (upper side turret)
Motor:	Perkins Condor 12 V 12-cylinder diesel
Efficiency kW/hp:	883/1200
Power/weight ratio:	19.2 hp/tonne
Top speed:	56 km/hr (road)
Fuel capacity:	1592 litres
Range:	450 km (without 2 x 200 litre supplementary tanks at rear)
Crew:	4
Armament:	1 x 120-mm L/30 cannon 1 x 7.62-mm coaxial MG, 1 x 7.62 mm AA MG 2 x 5 smoke mortars
Armour:	Steel armour, Dorchester compound armour, ERA optional
Fording depth:	1.07 metres: 4.57 m with snorkel

A Challenger 2 of the 1st Mechanized Brigade after taking part in a Royal Marines landing exercise. Browndown Beach, Gosport, Hampshire, England, 28 October 2010. (UK MoD)

A Challenger 2 at speed during an exercise on the British training grounds at Suffield, Canada. (UK MoD)

This Challenger 2 of the Queen's Royal Lancers is seen crossing an improvised bridge over a trench at the Kuwaiti-Iraqi border on 21 March 2003. As its predecessor twelve years before, the tank has supplementary armour at the front and sides. (UK MoD)

best protected of all armoured vehicles. In case of need, additional reactive and passive armour elements can be added. With its fully stabilized cannon and very modern fire-control system, thermal imaging unit, passive night vision apparatus and laser-rangefinder, the CR2 can detect its targets even at night and in poor visibility with a high first-round-hit probability. Like its predecessor, the CR2 can create smoke by spraying diesel fuel into the exhaust.

The CR2 had its baptism of fire during the Iraq War in 2003, equipped with sand filters, additional armour and anti-dust aprons. A CR2 bogged down in a roadside ditch was hit by no less than 14 RPG-7 anti-tank rockets and a *Milan* anti-tank missile. The crew remained unscathed, only the optics received damage. After being towed free by a recovery tank, within six hours the CR2 had been repaired and was operational again. Only one CR2 was a total loss in Iraq – as a result of friendly fire.

A Challenger 2 near Basra. The skirts at the turret sides are CIP (Combat Identification Panels) used for infra-red friend-foe recognition. Irak, March/April 2003. (UK MoD)

In 2004 within the framework of the CLIP-programme (*Challenger Lethality Improvement Programme*) trials were made with other cannons. Ultimately the choice fell on the 120-mm smooth-bore L/55 of the *Leopard* 2A6, mounted experimentally in a *Challenger 2* in 2006. Although it was intended in 2008 to re-equip all CR2s with the new cannon, install a new anti-NBC system and carry out other minor changes, budget restrictions intervened and in 2012 the plan was apparently cancelled. Since the end of 2007 however, numerous CR2 were given the *Street Fighter* modification involving the fitting of a remote-controlled weapons station on the turret roof, additional modular armour to the hull and turret sides, grille protection at the rear, a thermal imaging unit for the driver, a rear-view camera and an IED-jammer for the remote detonation of concealed explosive devices. This configuration, known unofficially as *Megatron*, weighs over 72 tonnes. 33 models each of the bridgelaying tank *Titan* and the pioneer tank *Trojan* were built based on the CR2. The armoured recovery tank CRARRV (*Challenger Armoured Repair and Recovery Vehicle*) did not proceed beyond the prototype stage. The only export client for the *Challenger 2* has been Oman, which bought 38 modified versions for desert operations. The special export variant *Challenger 2E* with a 1500 hp-MTU diesel and RENK automatic transmission could not compete on the international market against the *Leopard 2* and was withdrawn.

CR2 in the Street Fighter configuration, known unofficially as Megatron, seen at Bovington in June 2011 and June 2012. (Paul Appleyard)

Arjun

In 1974 India initiated its own domestic programme of battle tank development. The *Arjun* was developed in cooperation with numerous internal and international firms through the Indian Army's *Combat Research and Development Centre*, and the prototype was ready in 1984. Pre-series vehicles followed in 1987. Although it was planned to introduce the type at the beginning of the 1990s, series production was held back by reason of changing priorities and a host of problems, in particular those caused by the locally manufactured drive units and fire-control installation. Finally in 2000 the Indian Army ordered 124 *Arjun's* but these were not delivered until 2007. The tank has a fully stabilized 120-mm rifled cannon with thermal jacket for the barrel and a field adjustment installation loaded manually. The very modern computerized fire-control system provides a high first-round-hit probability. Protection comes from Kanchan compound armour developed in India *which* in trials withstood hits from a T72M1 125-mm cannon. Because the engine unit developed in India proved too unreliable, the 1400-hp MTU diesel and RENK automatic transmission imported from Germany were fitted in the series-run vehicles. The (Diehl) tank tracks were also imported initially from Germany, but are now manufactured under licence in India.

Type:	Arjun Mk I
Manufacturer:	HVF Avadi
Battle weight:	58,500 kg
Length:	10,638 mm (with barrel)
Breadth:	3864 mm (with aprons)
Height:	2320 mm (upper side turret), 3030 with air defence MG
Motor:	MTU 838 Ka 501 10-cylinder turbo diesel
Efficiency kW/hp:	1030/1400
Power/weight ratio:	29.93 hp/tonne
Top speed:	72 km/hr (road)
Fuel capacity:	1610 litres (additional tanks possible at rear)
Range:	450 km
Crew:	4
Armament:	1 x 120-mm cannon 1 x 7.62-mm coaxial MG, 1 x 12.7 mm AA MG 2 x 9 smoke mortars
Armour:	Steel armour, Kanchan compound armour, ERA optional
Fording depth:	1.4 metres

The decades-long development process, beset by problems, led to India going over to building the T-72 and then the T-90 today under licence. Although

One of the Arjun protoypes at an exhibition in New Delhi. (DRDO)

The Arjun programme was plagued by many problems and it is assumed that production will be terminated before even 250 series vehicles have been completed. (Indian Defence Ministry)

according to Indian sources trials in 2008/2009 to compare the T-90 against the *Arjun* resulted in the clear superiority of the latter, the programme will probably be terminated after the second batch of 124 *Arjun*'s (Mk II) is completed and, as has been made known, India will concentrate on manufacturing the T-90 under licence.

The *Arjun* Mk II was developed with Israeli assistance and, as has been reported, will have an engine developed in India, better optics, a laser warning system, an improved battle cannon with the capability of firing the Israeli laser-guided LAHAT missile, a remote-controlled weapons station on the turret roof, additional armour and a fitment for attaching an anti-landmine plough. Despite all these extra systems, it is hoped to keep the weight of the tank down to 55 tonnes. Testing of the Mk II began in June 2012, series production was scheduled to commence on successful completion of the tests, and the first tanks were issued to the units in 2014.

Under the designation *Tank Ex* at least two modified T-72 hulls (amongst other changes fitted with a new 1000-hp diesel) were given modified *Arjun* turrets for experimental purposes to see whether it would be possible to upgrade the Indian T-72 fleet. However, as at 2012 the armoured howitzer *Bhima* (with a 155-mm howitzer developed in South Africa) and armoured bridge-laying and recovery vehicles built on the basis of the *Arjun* had not emerged from the experimental stage.

T-72M1 Asad Babil

The *Asad Babil* (Lion of Babylon) was the Iraqi version of the T-72M1. At the beginning of the 1980s, Iraq had plans to produce the type under licence, but apparently by 1989/1990 less than 300 vehicles had been assembled from prefabricated Polish parts. The differences between *Asad Babil* and the original were minor. The *Asad Babil* had additional *schott* armour to the hull and front of the turret and was fitted with an electro-optic device of Chinese provenance for disrupting the flight of incoming anti-tank projectiles. The Iraqis also made minor changes to the chassis. Some of the tanks had a device attached to the exhaust enabling the tank to dig into the desert sand by the pressure of the expelled gases.

Apart from the Saladin Division, *Asad Babil* only saw action with units of the Republican Guard. Both in 1991 and 2003 they were outclassed by Allied battle tanks of the types M1 *Abrams* and *Challenger* 1 and 2.

Type:	T-72M1 Asas Babil
Manufacturer:	Nishni Tagil Tank Works (development), Iraqi Army Workshops (assembly and modifications)
Battle weight:	43,500 kg
Length:	6950 mm (hull), 9533 mm (with barrel)
Breadth:	3590 mm (with aprons)
Height:	2190 mm (without AA gun)
Motor:	W-46 12-cylinder diesel
Efficiency kW/hp:	574/780
Power/weight ratio:	17.93 hp/tonne
Top speed:	65 km/hr (road)
Fuel capacity:	1200 litres (internal)
Range:	450 km (600 km with 2 x 200 litre additional tanks at rear)
Crew:	3
Armament:	1 x 125-mm 2A46 cannon 1 x 7.62-mm coaxial MG, 1 x 12.7 mm AA MG 12 smoke mortars
Armour:	Steel armour, compound armour
Fording depth:	1.8 metres, 5 metres with snorkel

An artist's impression of the Asad Babil, the Iraqi version of the T-72M1. (Vincent Bourguignon)

Zufiqar

The *Zufiqar* (Sword of the Caliph Ali) is the first tank to have been developed in Iran. Previously Iran used imported M47/48/60s and *Chieftains*, T-54/55/72s and Type 59/69. The new development began in 1990: the first prototypes underwent testing in 1993, the pre-series following in 1997. Series production commenced in 1999. The chassis of the first version (*Zufiqar 1*) was based on that of the M48/60 with six roller wheels, the angular, welded 2-man turret equipped with 125-mm smooth bore cannon and automatic loading carousel was copied from the T-72. The fire-control unit came from Slovenia and was also included in the Iranian *Safir* 74 (modernized Type 59) and T-72Z (not a T-72, but a modernized T-55). The 780 hp diesel had further developed M60 transmission. According to Iranian sources, the tank was protected by their own design of compound armour and ERA.

The *Zufiqar 2* never advanced beyond the prototype, *Zufiqar 3* introduced in 2010 is basically a completely new tank, fitted with a new fire-control system, reinforced armour, new chassis, laser warning system and laser-rangefinder, a 1000 hp diesel, new turret and an altered hull form. Precise production figures are not available, but it is known that in 2001 Iran reportedly had around 100 *Zufiqar 1*s.

Type:	Zulfiqar 3
Manufacturer:	Shahid Kolah Dooz Industrial Complex
Battle weight:	c. 50 tonnes
Length:	c. 7 metres
Breadth:	c. 3.6 metres
Height:	c. 2.5 metres
Motor:	12-cylinder turbo-diesel (probably based on the AVDS-M60)
Efficiency kW/hp:	735/1000
Power/weight ratio:	c. 24.4 hp/tonne
Top speed:	70 km/hr (road)
Fuel capacity:	Not known, possibility exists for additional tanks at rear
Range:	c. 400-500 km
Crew:	3
Armament:	1 x 125-mm cannon 1 x 7.62-mm coaxial MG, 1 x 12.7 mm and 1 x 7.62 mm AA MG 1 x 12.7 MG above the cannon 2 x 4 smoke mortars
Armour:	Steel armour, compound armour, optional ERA
Fording depth:	Not known

The Zufiqar 3 is the newest version of this type of tank and has seven roller wheels with track guard. Hull and turret are reminiscent of the M1 Abrams US tank. (Vincent Bourguignon)

Magach

Tanks of Type M48/60 of improved fighting value, manufactured by IDF and designated *Magach* were procured during the 1960s and 1970s by Israel not only from the USA, but also the Federal Republic of Germany (around 150 M48A2) and captured vehicles in 1967 from Jordan. After the Six Day War of 1967 all M48s were converted to the 105-mm cannon and fitted with AVDS-1790-2A diesel motors, given a lower commander's cupola, new air filters, transmission and wireless equipment. The M48s (originally *Magach* 1 & 2) were redesignated *Magach* 3 after the modifications. M48A5 became *Magach* 5 but was barely distinguishable from the *Magach* 3 version. Magach 3 was used intensively during the Yom Kippur War of 1973 and some of them were fitted with Blazer reactive armour from the beginning of the 1980s. Modernized M60/M60A1 and A3s after being equipped with lower commander cupolas and receiving Blazer reactive armour (from the beginning of the 1980s) were redesignated *Magach* 6, a type which had at least nine sub-variants involving in particular improvements to engine and the fire-control installation. Most striking of these sub-variants is *Magach* 6B *Gal Batash* with its 908 hp diesel and both passive and reactive armour on the hull, turret and track guards which give the tank a completely new appearance. *Magach* 7 (from 1988)

Type:	Magach 7
Manufacturer:	IDF Ordnance Corps
Battle weight:	55 tonnes
Length:	6950 mm (hull)
Breadth:	3750 mm (with lateral aprons)
Height:	3250 mm (upper side turret)
Motor:	Continental VDS-1790-6A 12-cylinder diesel
Efficiency kW/hp:	668/908
Power/weight ratio:	16.51 hp/tonne
Top speed:	50 km/hr (road)
Fuel capacity:	1420 litres
Range:	450 km
Crew:	4
Armament:	1 x 105-mm M68 L/51 cannon 1 x 7.62-mm MG, 1 x 12.7 mm on the cannon 1 to 2 x 7.62 mm AA MG 1 x 60 mm mortar 2 x 6 smoke mortars
Armour:	max 254 mm steel armour, modular compound armour
Fording depth:	1.22 metres

Magach 6B with the second-generation Blazer reactive armour as operational at the end of the 1980s. (IMI)

A Magach 7C, recognizable by the wedge-shaped turret front, in the Yad la-Shiryon Museum, Israel 2005. (Bukvoed, cc by sa 2.5)

also has the 908 hp diesel and comprehensive additional compound armour but ERA tiles no longer. It received in addition a new fire-control system and *Merkava* tracks. The 7A version can be recognized by its relatively straight turret front whereas the 7C has a wedge-shaped turret front. Variant 7B was only a transitional tank and few examples were built.

More recently *Magach* 6 and 7 were used operationally primarily in Palestinian areas such as South Lebanon where they came under heavy fire from time to time. Thus in a Hezbollah ambush in the autumn of 1997, a 7A was hit by at least 20 AT-3 Sagger anti-tank missiles (9K11 *Maljutka*) of which two penetrated the armour, but only because they were fired from a hill downwards into the thin armour of the turret upper side. Some *Magach*'s also fell victim to explosive traps containing up to 100 kg explosive. Since 2006, all *Magach*'s have been transferred to reserve units. At present the IDF still has around 700 *Magach* 6 and 185 *Magach* 7.

The turret of the Magach 7A had a relatively straight front however. (IDF)

Merkava I and II

As soon as the Six Day War of 1967 ended, the Israelis began to consider having their own tank design. The final impetus for their *Merkava* ("fighting vehicle") was the high casualty rate amongst their tank troops in the Yom Kippur War in 1973. The first priority therefore became the protection of the crew, firepower and mobility was secondary. In order to minimize the development risks and simplify the logistics, the new tank would have components of the serving M48/60s and *Centurions*. A first prototype was exhibited in 1974, and the troops received the issue of the series vehicle in 1979. The *Merkava* first saw action in the fighting in Lebanon in 1982 which confirmed its concept, and although seven were destroyed there were no deaths amongst the crews. The engine and transmission are located forward in the welded cast-steel parts of the existing hull, thus serving as additional protection against hits to the front. The driver's position is inclined well back. A fuel tank is situated behind the nose of the hull, and behind it is a second armoured bulkhead. The turret sides also have *schott* armour. Having the drive unit forward creates space at the stern of the hull for additional ammunition or radio equipment, or sufficient room for infantry or wounded. The access

Type:	Merkava II
Manufacturer:	MATAK/IDF Ordnance Corps
Battle weight:	63 tonnes
Length:	7450 mm (hull), 8630 mm (with barrel)
Breadth:	3720 mm (with aprons)
Height:	2750 mm (commander's cupola)
Motor:	Continental AVDS 1790 6A 12-cylinder diesel
Efficiency kW/hp:	668/908
Power/weight ratio:	14.41 hp/tonne
Top speed:	48 km/hr (road)
Fuel capacity:	1250 litres
Range:	400 km
Crew:	4
Armament:	1 x 105-mm cannon M68 L/51 1 x 7.62-mm coaxial MG, some with 1 x 12.7 mm on the cannon 2 x 7.62 mm air defence MG 1 x 60 mm mortar 2 x 6 smoke mortars
Armour:	steel armour, schott layered, Merkava ID with modular compound armour
Fording depth:	1.4 metres, 2 metres with preparation

This photograph of a Merkava 1 was taken on 27 August 2011 at the Museum of Military Technology, Lesany, Czech Republic. (Tom 733, cc by sa 3.0)

A very early Merkava 1, taken in 1978 during the celebrations for the 30th anniversary of the founding of the State of Israel. It was the designers' philosophy that if possible every building component should contribute towards crew protection. At the centre rear is the drop-door for entry and at its sides the access slots for the batteries (left) and the anti-NBC protection (right). (IDF)

The Merkava IID was fitted later with modular compound armour to turret and hull. The intention of having tracks weighted with bullets hanging from the turret rear was to detonate incoming hollow-charge projectiles prematurely to protect this sensitive area. The grilled basket at the turret rear serves the same purpose. (Vincent Bourguignon)

hatch here has a two-part horizontal door with upper and lower flaps. This door simplifies the procedure to leave the vehicle under fire. The wedge-shaped turret is of cast steel with welded front. The main weapon is a fully-stabilized 105-mm rifled barrel M68 with thermal jacket for the barrel. An addition to the usual MGs (coaxial and anti-aircraft) is a 60-mm mortar. The digital fire-control installation has a laser rangefinder providing a high first-round-hit probability. From ahead the turret offers only a very narrow target and also has *schott* armour.

The Merkava chassis is unusual for a modern battle tank because the coil springs are fitted outside the hull. This system is rather like the Horstmann chassis of the Centurion and enables quick replacement in the event of damage, for the springs are easy to obtain and as fitted externally provide an additional element of protection. The undercarriage and hull sides are also protected by lateral aprons.

In the Lebanese War of 1982 the *Merkava* proved its worth by destroying several modern Syrian T-72 without losses to its own type. *Merkava* II introduced in 1983 is based on the battle experience of the *Merkava* in 1982 and has an improved fire-control installation and a new Israeli-built engine and transmission, and a 60-mm mortar in the turret. The IIB version was fitted with a thermal imaging unit, the type IIC was given additional armour on the roof. The turret and hull of variant IID (also II *Dor Dalef*) was fitted from the end of the 1990s with modular compound armour which substantially altered the profile. In contrast to version II meanwhile, Merkava I no longer has a place with the frontline troops, and is kept with the reserve units. Altogether 250 *Merkava* I and 580 *Merkava* II have been built.

A Merkava II of the Israeli Israeli Defence Force (IDF) during a manouevre. The absence of the side apron reveals details of the wheels and suspension, particularly the exterior fitted coil springs. Israel, 28 February 2012. (IDF)

Merkava III and IV

The series production of *Merkava* III, already fitted with modular compound armour, began at the end of 1989. The model was given a 1200 hp diesel and an Israeli-developed 120-mm smooth bore L/44 cannon with improved fire-control installation, laser warning system and other changes of a minor nature. The IIIB version has improved armour, the IIIBAZ an improved fire-control system with stabilized optics, a new anti-NBC system with air conditioning and a rear view camera. Some vehicles of the model were adapted for urban operations and fitted with anti-splinter optics, 360° external cameras and a bullet shield in the stern door. From the sub-variant IIID onwards new compound armour elements (similar to the IID version) and improved tracks were fitted.

Merkava IV has been manufactured since 2004. It has new modular compound armour above a 1500 hp General Dynamics diesel built under MTU licence, and RENK automatic transmission produced in Israel under licence. To accommodate this drive unit it was necessary to redesign the hull. The IV also has a redesigned turret with improved 120-mm cannon, a new fire-control system, improved anti-NBC system, a commander's independent optic with thermal

Type:	Merkava IV
Manufacturer:	MATAK/IDF Ordnance Corps
Battle weight:	65 tonnes
Length:	7600 mm (hull), 9040 mm (with barrel)
Breadth:	3720 mm (with aprons)
Height:	2890 mm (without air defence MG)
Motor:	GD 833 (MTU 833) 12-cylinder diesel
Efficiency kW/hp:	1103/1500
Power/weight ratio:	23.1 hp/tonne
Top speed:	64 km/hr (road)
Fuel capacity:	1400 litres
Range:	500 km
Crew:	4
Armament:	1 x 120-mm MG253 L/44 cannon 1 x 7.62-mm coaxial MG, some with 1 x 12.7 mm on the cannon 1 x 7.62 mm air defence MG 1 x 60 mm mortar 2 x 6 smoke mortars
Armour:	steel armour, modular compound armour
Fording depth:	1.4 metres, 2 metres with preparation

An early Merkava III with 120-mm cannon and lacking the additional armour which came later. Note how deep the tank sinks into the ground. (IDF)

A Merkava IIID BAZ of 188 Armoured Brigade firing live ammunition during manouevres. Beside conventional munitions the Merkava can also fire laser-directed LAHAT missiles. Golan Heights, 20 March 2008. (IDF)

Front profile of a Merkava IIID. (Michael Mass, cc by sa 3.0)

imaging, exterior cameras and network battlefield management system. The cannon is semi-automatic, fed from a 10-round magazine. The *Merkava* IV was given additional protection to combat the danger from anti-tank missiles aimed at its the upper surfaces (*Top Attack Weapons*). The designers also removed the gun-loader's hatch, since this presented a weak point in the turret roof armour.

Although the *Merkava* is counted amongst the most progressive and best protected battle tanks, in 2006 Hezbollah destroyed a fair number with modern anti-tank missiles during the Israeli incursion into Lebanon. As a counter-measure all *Merkava* IV are now fitted with a proximity-activated *Trophy* protection system (called *Windbreaker* by the IDF) which detects incoming missiles by radar and knocks them out with a charge of small shot. The system is also capable of calculating from where the missile was fired so that the tank crew can react quickly to engage the origin of the threat.

Merkava IV at the Yad la-Shiryon Museum, Israel, 2008. (Zachi Evinor)

This Merkava IV of 401 Armoured Brigade is fitted on both sides of the turret with the Windbreaker Hard-Kill system. Golan Heights, 11 February 2007. (IDF)

780 *Merkava* III and (up to the spring of 2012) 360 *Merkava* IV had been built, and another 300 of Type IV are scheduled to follow. On the basis of the *Merkava* an armoured howitzer (*Sholef*, only prototypes), a recovery vehicle (*Nemmera*) and a heavy infantry-tank (*Namer*) were also turned out.

OF-40

Between 1974 and 1983, OTO Melara built 720 *Leopard* 1 but could not export the type because of the tight restrictions of the West German licence. Therefore from 1977 OTO developed in concert with FIAT (competent for the drive elements) the model OF-40 (O for OTO, F for FIAT and 40 for the weight in tonnes aimed for) a tank which had a definite *Leopard* look about it. The first prototypes of the conventional model appeared in 1980 with a MTU diesel built by FIAT under licence and a 105-mm rifled barrel L7A3, but lacking a modern fire-control system and stabilized gun. Despite the comparatively favourable price, the UAE was the only client. After eighteen OF-40 in 1981, another batch of eighteen followed in 1985 together with three recovery vehicles on the same basis. This second batch had a digital fire-control installation with laser rangefinder and low light level camera above the now stabilized cannon. The first batch was subsequently upgraded to this standard. On the basis of the OF-40 the prototype of an air-defence tank with a 76-mm gun, and the howitzer-tank *Palmaria* were produced. The latter enjoyed a certain degree of export success and was purchased in some numbers by Libya (210), Nigeria (25) and Argentina (25).

Type:	OF-40
Manufacturer:	OTO Melara
Battle weight:	45,500 kg
Length:	6893 mm (hull) 9220 mm (with barrel)
Breadth:	3510 mm (with aprons)
Height:	2450 mm (upper side turret)
Motor:	MTU MB 838 Ca M500 10-cylinder diesel
Efficiency kW/hp:	610/830
Power/weight ratio:	18.24 hp/tonne
Top speed:	60 km/hr (road)
Fuel capacity:	1000 litres
Range:	600 km
Crew:	4
Armament:	1 x 105-mm L7A3 L/51 cannon 1 x 7.62-mm coaxial MG, 1 x 12.7 mm or 1 x 7.62 mm air defence MG 2 x 4 smoke mortars
Armour:	max 80 mm steel armour
Fording depth:	1.2 metres, 4 metres with snorkel

Although the OF-40 looks like the Leopard 1A4, it is actually an independent design. The variant OF-40/120 MK 2A with 120-mm cannon and 1000 hp diesel introduced in 1993 never made it past the protoype stage. (Vincent Bourguignon)

Ariete

In 1984 IVECO and OTO Melara formed a consortium (CIO) to develop a range of new vehicles including a modern battle tank for the Italian military. OTO agreed responsibility for hull, turret and armament, IVECO for the motor unit. The first prototypes were exhibited in 1986 but the armoured brigades did not receive the issue until 1995. The *Ariete* (Ram) has compound armour and the typical appearance of a modern Western battle tank. It has a 120-mm smooth bore L/44 cannon, a digital state-of-the-art fire-control system with thermal imaging, laser rangefinder and stabilized optics. The layout is conventional, the driver being seated centrally forward in the hull, the other three crew members having their places in the turret. The 1250-hp diesel drive is situated at the rear. By 2012 the Italian Army had received a total of 200 *Ariete*. The vehicles were originally designated C-1 since a C-2 version with 1500-hp motor, hydropneumatic suspension, automatic loader and improved armour was expected to follow. It was shelved, and so the C-1 designation fell away. The existing tanks were given new 1600-hp IVECO diesels and fitted with additional armour.

Type:	Ariete
Manufacturer:	OTO Melara and IVECO consortium (CIO)
Battle weight:	54 tonnes
Length:	7590 mm (hull) 9669 mm (with barrel)
Breadth:	3601 mm (with aprons)
Height:	2500 mm (upper side turret)
Motor:	IVECO V-12 MTCA 838 12-cylinder diesel
Efficiency kW/hp:	919/1250
Power/weight ratio:	23.15 hp/tonne
Top speed:	65+ km/hr (road)
Fuel capacity:	1100 litres
Range:	550-600 km
Crew:	4
Armament:	1 x 120-mm L/44 cannon 1 x 7.62-mm coaxial MG, 1 x 7.62 mm air defence MG 2 x 4 smoke mortars
Armour:	steel armour, compound armour, ERA optional
Fording depth:	1.2 metres, 3 metres with snorkel

This photograph of an Ariete battle tank was taken at an Italian Army exhibition in Rome on 4 November 2010. (Kaminski, cc by sa 3.0)

For operations in Iraq the tanks were fitted with additional armour at the sides of the hull (and parts of the turret sides). Operation Antica Babilonia, Task Force Pegaso, Iraq, 15 July 2003-1 December 2006. (Vincent Bourguignon)

An Ariete in heavy terrain. (OTO Melara)

Type 74

The first plans for the Type 74 were laid in the early 1960s, prototypes followed in 1968/69. Though equipped with an automatic loader and remote-operated AA gun, these features were discontinued later. The first series-vehicles came off the line in 1975, the production terminated in 1989 after the 893rd. The Type 74 is basically of conventional design but with interesting characteristics. Most Western battle tanks of its generation have roller wheels with torsion bar suspension. The Type 74 on the other hand has five large running wheels and hydropneumatic suspension which render the rollers superfluous . This type of chassis with automatic transmission allows the driver a ground clearance of between 20-60 cms, and additionally the Type 74 can be inclined forward or back (increasing the elevation/depression arc and traverse of the fully stabilized 105-mm rifled bore L7 cannon, built under licence). The fire-control system is digitalized and has a laser rangefinder. IR searchlights enable night operations to be carried out. An anti-NBC system is also available. In the course of production some changes of details

Type:	Type 74
Manufacturer:	Mitsubishi Heavy Industries
Battle weight:	38 tonnes
Length:	6700 (hull) 9420 mm (with barrel)
Breadth:	3180 mm
Height:	2480 mm (upper side turret), 2670 mm (with AA gun)
Motor:	Mitsubishi 10ZF Zyp 22 WT 10-cylinder diesel
Efficiency kW/hp:	530/720
Power/weight ratio:	18.94 hp/tonne
Top speed:	60 km/hr (road)
Fuel capacity:	950 litres
Range:	400 km
Crew:	4
Armament:	1 x 105-mm L/51 L7 cannon 1 x 7.62-mm coaxial MG 1 x 12.7-mm AA MG 2 x 3 smoke mortars
Armour:	max. 120 mm steel armour
Fording depth:	1 metre, 2 metres with preparation

Display of a Type 74 at Tsuchiura, Kanto, Japan in October 2007. A mine clearance/excavating shield can be attached at the front. (Max Smith)

The hydropneumatic suspension enables the Type 74 to alter its ground clearance forward or at the stern. (JGSDF)

The low, ballistically favourable shape of the Type 74 can be clearly seen from this photograph. The large IR searchlight is at the left of the cannon. Narashino, Japan, 13 January 2008. (PD)

were undertaken (variants A to F), but the only major modification (to Type 74 *Kai* or Type 74G) was abandoned in 1994 on the grounds of cost after only four tanks had been converted. Besides IR cameras and track aprons this version has been given modular additional armour and a laser warning system. An air

defence tank (Type 87), a bridgelayer (Type 91) and a recovery vehicle (Type 78) were all built on the basis of the Type 74. According to the latest planning, the around 300 Type 74s still in service in 2012 are to be replaced in stages by the Type 10.

Type 90

The Japanese Army knew at the introduction of the Type 74 that it already lagged behind the times, and so in the mid-1970s work began on a fighting vehicle to match the Soviet T-72. The first prototypes were completed in 1982, another four experimental vehicles followed between 1984 and 1986. The model was accepted officially by the Japanese forces in 1990, and the first series-tanks arrived at the units in 1992. The Type 90 has modern compound armour protection which gives the tank the typical shape of contemporary Western battle tanks. The armour is modular at the front of the tank. The main weapon is a Rheinmetall 120-mm smooth bore L/44 cannon built under licence and of the type also fitted to the *Leopard* 2, M1 *Abrams* or the Korean K1, but in contrast the Type 90 cannon is fed ammunition by an automatic loader at the rear of the turret which allows a reduction in crew numbers to three and a smaller turret. The first and last running wheels have hydropneumatic suspension while the middle six have torsion bars. This allows the hull of the Type 90 to be inclined forward or back, though not sideways

Type:	Type 90
Manufacturer:	Mitsubishi Heavy Industries
Battle weight:	50 tonnes
Length:	7500 mm (hull) 9755 mm (with barrel)
Breadth:	3430 mm (with aprons)
Height:	2340 mm (upper side turret
Motor:	Mitsubishi 10ZG 10-cylinder diesel
Efficiency kW/hp:	1103/1500
Power/weight ratio:	30 hp/tonne
Top speed:	70+ km/hr (road)
Fuel capacity:	1101 litres
Range:	350 km
Crew:	3
Armament:	1 x 120-mm L/44 cannon 1 x 7.62-mm coaxial MG 1 x 12.7-mm AA MG 2 x 4 smoke mortars
Armour:	steel armour, compound armour, partly modular
Fording depth:	2 m

A Type 90 during an exhibition at Tsuchiura, Kano, Japan in October 2007. (Max Smith)

Like the Type 74, the Type 90 is able to low its ground clearance forward or astern. Hokkaido, Japan, 2009. (16DDHhyuga, cc by sa 3.0)

as with the Type 74. The driver can additionally vary the ground clearance (even on the move) between 20 and 60 cms. The digitalized fire-control installation with thermal imaging, laser rangefinder and crosswind sensor correspond to the most modern requirements, and were assessed on numerous occasions during the course of manufacture. The Type 90 has a laser warning system which upon detecting a threat discharges smoke grenades automatically. Although it is a very mobile, well protected and modern battle tank, the Type 90 was not exported due to Government policy restrictions. By 2009 a total of 341 Type 90s had left the assembly halls. Recovery tanks (Type 90 ARV) and bridgelayers (Type 91 AVLB) were also built on the basis of the Type 90.

Type 10

The development of a new battle tank to replace the Type 74 and complement the Type 90 began at the end of the 1990s. Because of its relatively heavy weight, the Japanese Army did not consider the Type 90 suitable for all areas of the mountainous islands of Japan and therefore limited its operational area to the island of Hokkaido. The objective of the new development was therefore a lighter battle tank of which the mountainous infrastructure (narrow roads, bridges with limited weight-bearing capacity) did not ask too much. The prototype was displayed in February 2008, and the Japanese Government at first ordered 13 series-built tanks which were received by the units at the beginning of 2012. The Type 10 may be considered at present as the most modern battle tank and has a number of interesting features. The five large running wheels with hydropneumatic suspension enable the driver to adjust the ground clearance and incline the hull in all directions,and the modular compound armour of the most modern kind is also striking. In the basic armour format the Type

Type:	Type 10
Manufacturer:	Mitsubishi Heavy Industries
Battle weight:	40 to 48 tonnes
Length:	9420 mm (with barrel)
Breadth:	3240 mm (with aprons)
Height:	2300 mm (upper side turret)
Motor:	Mitsubishi 8-cylinder diesel
Efficiency kW/hp:	883/1200
Power/weight ratio:	25-30 hp/tonne
Top speed:	70+ km/hr (road)
Fuel capacity:	n/a
Range:	n/a
Crew:	3
Armament:	1 x 120-mm L/44 cannon 1 x 7.62-mm coaxial MG 1 x 12.7-mm AA MG smoke mortars
Armour:	steel armour, compound armour, partly modular
Fording depth:	n/a

The Japanese Army received its first series-built Type 10 tanks at the beginning of 2012. This example attached to 1st Armoured Training Unit/Eastern Army Combined Brigade was photographed at Camp Takeyama, Japan on 27 May 2102. (PD)

Another view of the Type 10 in which the commander's optic, installed on its own "tower" and able to be moved through 360°, can be clearly seen. (PD)

10 weighs about 40 tonnes, but the addition of *schott* armour elements increase the weight to 44 tonnes. In full armour mode the total vehicular weight is 48 tonnes. In addition, not only the front is heavily armoured, but the all-round protection is correspondingly effective. When danger threatens or the tank is detected, a laser-, radar- and IR warning system discharges the smoke mortars automatically. Thanks to the infinitely variable speed transmission the tank can move as fast in reverse as forwards. The Type 10 has a fire-control and battlefield management system of the most modern design. The designers laid especial value on the C4ISR capability

(*Command and Control, Communications, Computers, Intelligence, Surveillance and Reconnaissance*). This gives the Type 10 the ability to exchange data linked into a network with similarly equipped tanks. The main weapon is an improved version of the 120-mm smooth-bore L/44 cannon built under licence for the Type 90, and with an automatic loader in the turret rear. The crew is therefore only three men. The 12.7-mm air defence MG can be aimed and fired from the interior. As there are around 300 Type 74s still in service with the Japanese Army, it may be assumed that a similar number of Type 10s will be produced.

Khalid

In 1972, Royal Ordnance received a contract from Iran to build 125 *Shir* 1 (FV 4030/2) and 1,225 *Shir* 2 (FV 4030/3), these being further developments of the *Chieftain*. The new Islamic Government of Iran cancelled this contract in 1979. At that time, production had already begun. At that, Jordan ordered 274 lightly modified FV 4030/2 as *Khalid*. This tank is basically a variant of the *Chieftain* but with different chassis, new transmission, a more efficient cooling system and a modern fire-control installation with prominent commander's optic and passive night vision apparatus. The major weakness of the *Chieftain*, its L60 motor, is replaced by a 1200-hp diesel also fitted in *Challenger 1*. For this purpose the rear of the hull had be redesigned to the extent that now it resembles the *Challenger 1*. The first *Khalid*'s were delivered in 1981 and remain in Jordanian service to the present day.

Type:	Khalid
Manufacturer:	Royal Ordnance
Battle weight:	58 tonnes
Length:	8390 mm (hull) 11550 mm (with barrel)
Breadth:	3518 mm (with aprons)
Height:	2975 mm
Motor:	Perkins Condor 12V 12-cylinder diesel
Efficiency kW/hp:	883/1200
Power/weight ratio:	20.68 hp/tonne
Top speed:	56 km/hr (road)
Fuel capacity:	950 litres
Range:	400 km
Crew:	4
Armament:	1 x 120-mm L11 A5 cannon 1 x 7.62-mm coaxial MG 1 x 7.62-mm AA MG 2 x 6 smoke mortars
Armour:	max. 185 mm steel armour
Fording depth:	1.07 m, 4.57 m with snorkel

This photograph of a Khalid was taken at the Bovington Tank Museum, England, in June 2011. (Paul Appleyard)

M-84

In 1979 the former Yugoslavia obtained rights to build the Soviet T-72A under licence, and the first series-vehicles were completed in 1984 (therefore M-84). The original M-84 was in many respects very similar to the Soviet original although the fire-control unit was replaced by one of Yugoslav design. In the course of time there were several M-84 variants. The M-84A has a 1000-hp diesel and improved fire-control system and optics, while the M-84AB was prioritized for desert regions and given minor improvements. Sub-variants of the M-84AB are a command tank (M-84ABK) with additional radio and D/F equipment: the M-84ABN has a navigational system. Until the break-up of Yugoslavia in 1992, around 450 M-84s were built for homeland requirements.

In 1989 Kuwait ordered over 170 M-84AB's and ABN's and 15 ABK's. Only a handful of these had been delivered by when Iraq invaded Kuwait. Kuwaiti units managed to escape to Saudi Arabia with 70 M-84AB's and took part in the re-conquest of their homeland. The tanks only returned there after the end of the war in Kuwait.

After the break-up of Yugoslavia in 1992 the M-84 was built in Serbia and also Croatia. Until then around

Type:	M84AB
Manufacturer:	Up until 1992 former Yugoslav State factory, today Duro Dakovic (Croatia) and Yugo-import SDPR (Serbia)
Battle weight:	42 tonnes
Length:	6860 mm (hull) 9530 mm (with barrel)
Breadth:	3570 mm (with aprons)
Height:	2190 mm (upper side turret)
Motor:	V-46TK 12-cylinder diesel
Efficiency kW/hp:	735/1000
Power/weight ratio:	23.8 hp/tonne
Top speed:	65 km/hr (road)
Fuel capacity:	1200 lites (2 x 200 litre additional tanks optional at rear)
Range:	700 km
Crew:	3
Armament:	1 x 125-mm 2A46 L/48 cannon 1 x 7.62-mm coaxial MG 1 x 12.7-mm AA MG 12 smoke mortars
Armour:	steel armour, compound armour
Fording depth:	1.2 m, 5m with snorkel

A Kuwaiti M-84 in the Saudi Arabian desert. In 1989 Kuwait ordered 170 M-84AB and 84ABN as well as 15 ABK's. By the time Iraq invaded Kuwait, only a handful of these tanks had been delivered. (US Army)

An M-84 of the Serb armoured forces. The relationship to the T-72 is evident. The M-84 was used frequently during the wars in Yugoslavia during the 1990s but was not thought of too highly since fair numbers of them were destroyed in action. (Serb Forces)

500 M-84s had been built for the Yugoslav Federal Army. They were used operationally during the Yugoslav civil wars of the 1990s when a fair number of them were destroyed.

Kuwaiti M-84s. Saudi Arabia, 1990. (US Army)

M-84A4 Sniper

After the break-up of Yugoslavia, Croatia developed the M-84A4 Sniper with modernized fire-control and communications equipment on the basis of the M-84. Between 1996 and 2003 forty new *Snipers* were built by Croatia. Up to 2008 an additional 44 old M-84s were modernized to this standard. Slovenia converted 54 M-84s to the A-4 standard. Reports that the vehicles were fitted with German 1100-hp diesels remained unconfirmed. Croatia also developed the M-95 *Degman* based on the Yugoslav prototype M-91 *Vihor* but the project did not proceed beyond the experimental stage. The M-95 has a welded turret, new compound and ERA armour and numerous minor improvements.

The Croatian M-84D, though retaining the old cast steel M-84 turret, has new additional armour and many of the innovations intended for the M-95 including a remotely operated 12.7-mm air defence weapon, a laser warning system and the capability of firing the Israeli LAHAT missile. Croatia is also planning to upgrade six new M-84D to that standard. Some years ago Kuwait showed interest in the M-84D but nothing came of it. The technical details of the M-84A4 correspond to those of the basic model. The weight of the M-84D variant rose to 48.5 tons with the additional armour and the 1200-hp diesel was exchanged to lighten the burden.

The M-84D is a Croat version with various improvements, amongst them comprehensive additional armour. (Duro Dakovic)

Ch'onma-ho

During the 1970s and 1980s North Korea received a series of T-62s originating from the USSR and Syria. In 1978 North Korea began to build its own version of the T-62 given the name *Ch'onma* (Pegasus), *ho* (Type, model). Over the years the type was subjected to much upgrading, but the information tends to be contradictory and the type designations overlap. Some of the improvements included the equipping with laser rangefinder above the cannon, thermal barrel jacket, new optics and fire-control system, lateral aprons and both ERA and NERA additional armour at the front of the hull and turret. The V and VI versions are the most modern variants of this battle tank. After North Korea succeeded in obtaining some T-72s at the beginning of the 1990s, features of this tank now appeared in the *Ch'onma-ho*, and thus the V version has compound armour, a 125-mm smooth bore cannon with automatic loader, a modern fire-control system and other minor improvements. The VI may have newly reinforced armour. The total number of *Ch'onma-ho* manufactured in North Korea is not known. Estimates range from 1000 to 1400 which do service with probably around 800 imported T-62s presumably similarly upgraded.

Type:	Ch'onma-ho
Manufacturer:	North Korean State organisations
Battle weight:	c. 40 tonnes
Length:	c. 6600 mm (hull)
Breadth:	c. 3500 mm
Height:	c. 2400 mm (upper side turret)
Motor:	Diesel
Efficiency kW/hp:	c. 552/750
Power/weight ratio:	c. 18.75 hp/tonne
Top speed:	c. 50 km/hr (road)
Fuel capacity:	n/a (2 x 200 litre additional tanks at the rear optional)
Range:	c. 400-500 km (without additional tanks)
Crew:	4
Armament:	1 x 115 mm 2A20 L/55 or 125 mm 2A46 L/48 cannon 1 x 7.62 mm coaxial MG 1 x 12.7 or 14.5 mm AA MG smoke mortars
Armour:	steel armour, *Schott*, ERA and compound armour
Fording depth:	c. 1.4 m without, 5 m with snorkel

(Only estimated values can be provided on account of the North Korea's restricted information policy.)

The Ch'onma-ho is a modernized version of the T-62. This photograph was taken at a parade in Pyong-yang, April 2012. (US DoD)

P'okp'ung-ho

The *P'okp'ung-ho* (Storm Tiger-model) is presently the most modern North Korean tank. It has been known of since 2002, the development probably having begun in the later 1990s. It appeared in public for the first time in 2010. What is known of the vehicle is sparse and to some extent contradictory since it is based only on what North Korean State television chooses to reveal and by analyzing the only known photographs. Although the tracks and running wheels are very similar to the *Ch'onma-ho*, the *P'okp'ung-ho* has a longer hull with six instead of five rollers per side and seems to have been influenced by the T-72, although the driver sits forward left side as before whereas in the T-72 he sits in the centre. The engine room cover and hull rear on the other hand resemble the T-72. Since 2010 three versions of the tank have been recognized. The *P'okp'ung-ho* has striking additional protection at the front of turret and hull and to all appearances has a 115-mm smooth bore cannon like the earlier *Ch'onma-ho*. Whether the supplementary armour is compound material or a simple *schott* is not known. The *P'okp'ung-ho* has a cast steel turret with thickened front reminiscent of the T-72B which might be integral with the compound armour elements. This version has additional ERA tiles at the hull front and a 125-mm smooth bore cannon. The newest variant, *P'okp'ung-ho III* is the II version with additional ERA elements on the turret face. All three models have a laser

Type:	P'okp'ung-ho
Manufacturer:	North Korean State organisations
Battle weight:	c. 44 tonnes
Length:	c. 7200 mm (hull)
Breadth:	c. 3600 mm
Height:	c. 2500 mm (upper side turret)
Motor:	Diesel
Efficiency kW/hp:	c. 735/1000
Power/weight ratio:	c. 22.73 hp/tonne
Top speed:	c. 65 km/hr (road)
Fuel capacity:	n/a (2 x 200 litre additional tanks at rear optional)
Range:	c. 400-500 km (without additional tanks)
Crew:	3 or 4 (depending on whether automatic loader present)
Armament:	1 x 115 mm 2A20 L/55 or 125 mm 2A46 L/48 cannon 1 x 7.62 mm coaxial MG 1 x 14.5 mm AA MG 2 x 4 smoke mortars
Armour:	steel armour, *Schott*, ERA and compound armour
Fording depth:	c. 1.4 m without, 5 m with snorkel

(Only estimated values can be provided on account of the North Korea's restrictive information policy.)

Side profile of the P'okp'ung-ho I. (Vincent Bourguignon)

The newest version of the P'okp'ung-ho, the Mk III, displayed during a parade through Pyong-yang, April 2012.

rangefinder above the cannon and a crosswind sensor on the turret roof to go with the very modern digital fire-control system. The rear of the turret has a grille-type stowage basket providing additional protection against hollow-charge projectiles. The lateral aprons are flexible, maybe rubber with a metal inlay or other compound material. In the forward area four metal elements can be made out per side, whether these are simple steel plates, compound material or ERA tiles is unknown. The night fighting capability is still based on IR searchlights. It is not known if the

P'okp'ung-ho II and III like other tanks armed with the 125-mm cannon also have the automatic loader. Although a 1500-hp diesel was suspected initially, it appears now that the motor only produces 1000 hp. How many of these tanks have been built to date is not known. All in all, although the P'okp'ung-ho represents an impressive improvement over the other battle tanks in the North Korean Army, it is worlds away from the K1 and K2 of South Korea or the US forces' M1.

Al-Zarrar

Because the Pakistani Army had around 1200 Chinese Type 59 battle tanks, it was not possible financially to replace this large number of vehicles. Therefore in 1990 an upgrading programme was embarked upon. The tanks received a 125-mm smooth bore cannon with semi-automatic loader as fitted in the Type 85-IIAP and the *Al Khalid*. This not only increased the hitting power of the Type 59 but also simplified the logistics. Additions also came in the form of a new 730 hp diesel, a modern fire-control system with laser rangefinder, a laser warning system, improved running wheels and modular supplementary armour with elements of compound material and ERA. These Type 59 conversions were designated *Al-Zarrar* in Pakistan. Delivery to the units began in 2004. Since then a number of *Al-Zarrar* variants have been observed differing from one another in the turret shape. While some tanks are fitted with ERA elements to the old Type 59 cast steel turret, others seemed to have new, cornered welded turrets. This was a false impression, however, for pictures of *Al-Zarrars* wrecked in battle against the Taliban showed that they had only been given a thin *schott* armour over the original cast steel turrets. By 2010 around 400 *Al Zarrars* had been built.

Type:	Al-Zarrar
Manufacturer:	HIT (Heavy Industries Taxila)
Battle weight:	40 tonnes
Length:	6040 mm (without barrel)
Breadth:	3270 mm (without track aprons)
Height:	n/a
Motor:	V-12 diesel
Efficiency kW/hp:	382/730
Power/weight ratio:	18.25 hp/tonne
Top speed:	65 km/hr (road)
Fuel capacity:	n/a
Range:	450 km, (600 km with additional tanks at rear)
Crew:	4
Armament:	1 x 125 mm cannon 1 x 7.62 mm coaxial MG 1 x 12.7 mm AA MG
Armour:	steel armour, (20-203 mm) ERA, schott and compound armour
Fording depth:	c. 1.4 m, 4.8 m with snorkel

Al-Zarrar is the Pakistani designation for a comprehensive modernization of their old Chinese Type 59 tanks. (Pakistan Army)

Al Khalid

The *Al-Khalid* is based on the Chinese Type 90-II and has been built under licence in Pakistan in modified form since 2001. During the 1990s six protoypes built in China underwent intensive trials, differing principally in the engine unit: Chinese, German, British, French and Ukrainian diesels were tried. The Type 90-IIM version with a Ukrainian 1200 hp diesel and French automatic transmission came out on top in the hot, dry and dusty desert climate of southern Pakistan and was therefore adopted as the basis for the licensed model. The basic *Al-Khalid* has modular compound- and ERA protection. The main differences lie in a fire-control and cannon stabilizing installation of Western manufacture, a battlefield management system with data link, an inertial navigation installation with integral GPS and a laser warning system. The exact number of *Al-Khalids* built to date is unknown, but is probably between 250 and 300.

Al-Khalid I has been under test since 2009. It has a higher inventory of 125-mm shells (49 instead of 39), an automatic loader providing improved rate of fire, a better fire-control system, new thermal imaging device and other minor improvements.

Type:	Al-Khalid
Manufacturer:	HIT (Heavy Industries Taxila)
Battle weight:	48 tonnes
Length:	6900 mm (hull) 10067 mm (with barrel)
Breadth:	3500 mm
Height:	2400 mm (upper side turret)
Motor:	KMDB 6TD-2 6-cylinder opposed piston diesel
Efficiency kW/hp:	883/1200
Power/weight ratio:	25 hp/tonne
Top speed:	70 km/hr (road)
Fuel capacity:	n/a
Range:	450 km (internal tanks)
Crew:	3
Armament:	1 x 125 mm cannon 1 x 7.62 mm coaxial MG 1 x 12.7 mm AA MG 2 x 6 smoke mortars
Armour:	steel armour, compound armour, ERA
Fording depth:	c. 1.4 m, 5.0 m with snorkel

The Al Khalid is built in Pakistan but based on the Chinese Type 90-II. (Pakistan Army)

Pt-91 Twardy

The PT-91 is based on the T-72M1 built under licence in Poland. The development of the *Twardy* (Tough Nut) began at the beginning of the 1980s, the first prototypes were completed in 1992. The Polish Army received a total of 233 PT-91s between 1995 and 2002 as well as a number of pioneer-, recovery- and bridge-laying vehicles based on it. Main differences from the T-72MI (alongside many other minor modifications) are an improved digital fire-control system and cannon stabilizing installation, a low light level camera, a laser warning system, a more efficient engine and ERA developed in Poland. Although for example India adopted the fire-control system of the PT-91 for its T-72 modernization programme, Malaysia is to date the only export client for the PT-91, and received 48 battle- and 15 support-tanks between 2007 and 2009. The PT-91M *Pendekar* differs from the Polish model by its 1000-hp motor with new transmission, a French fire-control and stabilizing installation, new optics, an improved main weapon, stronger armour, new radio equipment, air conditioning and numerous other changes.

Type:	PT-91 Twardy
Manufacturer:	Bumar
Battle weight:	45,500 kg
Length:	6950 mm (hull) 9670 mm (with barrel)
Breadth:	3590 mm
Height:	2190 mm (upper side turret)
Motor:	S-12U 12-cylinder diesel
Efficiency kW/hp:	625/850
Power/weight ratio:	18.68 hp/tonne
Top speed:	60 km/hr (road)
Fuel capacity:	1000 litres
Range:	650 km (with internal tanks)
Crew:	3
Armament:	1 x 125 mm 2A46 L/48 cannon 1 x 7.62 mm coaxial MG 1 x 12.7 mm AA MG 2 x 12 smoke mortars
Armour:	steel armour, compound armour, ERA
Fording depth:	c. 1.4 m, 5.0 m with snorkel

The PT-91 is the Polish further development of the T-72. Notice the ERA and twelve smoke mortars per turret side. (Pibwl)

TR-77-580

In order to be independent of Soviet imports, in 1968 the Rumanian Government ordered a domestic-built battle tank. A first protoype was introduced in 1974. Although as a result of its lack of experience in the designing of tanks Rumanian industry used the T-55 for a model, the resulting article had far-reaching changes. Therefore the TR-77-580 (*Tanc Romanesc Model* 1977, 580 refers to the engine efficiency) had a longer hull with six rolling wheels on torsion bars per side protected by metal side aprons. The armour was reinforced, the turret enlarged and a Rumanian fire-control system used in conjunction with a 100-mm rifled bore A308 cannon based on the Rumanian A407 anti-tank gun. Export approval for the German 800 hp diesel wanted was not forthcoming: in its place recourse was had to the 580 hp engine of the T-55. Between 1979 and 1985 around 400 TR-77-580s were built, 150 of them going for export from 1982 to 1984. Officially the buyer was Egypt, but they made their way later to Iraq. Whether the type was used in the Iraq-Iran War or later conflicts is not known.

Type:	TR-77-580
Manufacturer:	ROMARM
Battle weight:	41 tonnes
Length:	9250 mm (with barrel)
Breadth:	3300 mm
Height:	2400 mm (upper side turret)
Motor:	V-55 12-cylinder diesel
Efficiency kW/hp:	437/580
Power/weight ratio:	14.15 hp/tonne
Top speed:	60 km/hr (road)
Fuel capacity:	n/a (2 x 200 litre supplementary tanks at rear optional)
Range:	400 km (with internal tanks)
Crew:	4
Armament:	1 x 100 mm A308 cannon 1 x 7.62 mm coaxial MG 1 x 12.7 mm AA MG 2 x 8 smoke mortars
Armour:	steel armour, (later models partly with schott armour)
Fording depth:	c. 1.4 m, 5.0 m with snorkel

A TR-77-580 of the Rumanian Forces. The first of them delivered to Egypt were much criticized in Press reports for their appalling lack of quality. (Rumanian Defence Ministry)

TR-85

The TR-85 (also TR-85-800 or only TR-800) was based on the TR-77-580. Series production of the TR-85 began in 1986 and by 1990 about 600 had been manufactured. The TR-85 had a new fire-control system with laser rangefinder and crosswind sensor developed in Rumania, cannon stabilization, revised track-and-wheels, and a "redesigned" copy of the *Leopard* MB 838 Ca M500 engine. In order to bring the TR-85 up to the NATO standard, in 1999 a modernisation programme was drawn up by which the Type received a revised motor, an improved fire-control installation with thermal imaging camera above the cannon, a laser warning system which automatically set off the smoke mortars should danger be detected, new APFSDS ammunition, a thermal barrel sleeve for the cannon, a rebuilt rear, passive additional armour and other minor changes. This model received the designation TR 85M1 *Bisonul* (Bison). Based on the TR-85 is a small number of pioneer- and recovery vehicles. The Rumanian Army has 249 TR-85s and 56 TR-85M1s.

From 1984 a domestic variant of the T-72 was produced in Rumania (TR-125) following the pattern

Type:	TR-85M1
Manufacturer:	ROMARM
Battle weight:	50 tonnes
Length:	6740 mm (hull) 9960 mm (with barrel)
Breadth:	3435 mm
Height:	2300 mm (upper side turret), 3100 mm (overall)
Motor:	8VS-A2T2M 8-cylinder diesel
Efficiency kW/hp:	633/860
Power/weight ratio:	17.2 hp/tonne
Top speed:	60 km/hr (road)
Fuel capacity:	1100 litres (2 x 200 litre supplementary tanks at rear optional)
Range:	400 km (on internal tanks)
Crew:	4
Armament:	1 x 100 mm A308 cannon 1 x 7.62 mm coaxial MG 1 x 12.7 mm AA MG 2 x 8 smoke mortars
Armour:	steel armour, compound and schott armour)
Fording depth:	c. 1.4 m, 5.0 m with snorkel

A TR-85 of 15.Mechanized Brigade. Seen in Rumania, 5 October 2011. (MAPN)

A TR-85M1 driving over the firing range at Miai Bravu during the Armaments Fair Expomil 2011. Rumania, September 2011. (Adrian Curiman/MAPN)

A TR-85 M1 (in the background an MLI-84M armoured troop-carrier) during the MILREX manouevres on 17 October 2007. Notice the new turret rear. (Petrica Mihalache/MAPN)

of the TR-77/TR-85, namely a lengthened hull with one additional running wheel per side, a motor based on the drive of the TR-85, reinforced protection, a fire-control installation developed in Rumania and a 125-mm smooth bore cannon. After three protoypes had been built the development was scrapped at the beginning of the 1990s on financial grounds.

Stridsvagn 122

Resulting from the Swedish Army's comparison trials of the T-80U, M1A2, *Leclerc* and *Leopard* 2A5 in 1993, the latter was declared the victor in 1994. Sweden then ordered 160 used tanks corresponding to the *Leopard 2A4* in all but minor details and then agreed with Krauss Maffei Wegmann the licenced production of the A5. The first 20 were delivered from Germany, another hundred were manufactured at Hägglunds and Bofors. The Swedish tanks differed fairly substantially from the German A5, the most noticeable being the use of MEXAS-additional armour at the front, an anti-bomblet protection for the turret roof and improved lateral aprons. Additionally there is a Swedish-built battlefield management system (TCCS-*Tank Command and Control System*), a GALIX smoke mortar installation and a modified fire-control computer. The motor-cooling unit was modified and the chassis adapted to take all this increased weight (62,5 tonnes). First deliveries followed in 1997 and production terminated in 2002. The version Strv 122B (until the present, 10 modified vehicles, weight 63.2 tonnes) has additional anti-landmine protection. In the future the Swedish Army will be introducing a more efficient version of the recovery tank *Büffel* ("Buffalo") (*Bärgningsbandvagn 120*).

Type:	Stridsvagn 122
Manufacturer:	Hägglunds and Bofors
Battle weight:	62,500 kg
Length:	7722 mm (hull) 9668 mm (with barrel)
Breadth:	3810 mm (with lateral aprons)
Height:	2640 mm
Motor:	MB 873-Ka 501 12-cylinder Vielstoff
Efficiency kW/hp:	1103/1500
Power/weight ratio:	24 hp/tonne
Top speed:	72 km/hr (road)
Fuel capacity:	1160 litres
Range:	460 km
Crew:	4
Armament:	1 x 120 mm L/44 cannon 1 x 7.62 mm coaxial MG3 1 x 7.62 mm AA MG3 2 x 9 smoke mortars
Armour:	steel armour, compound armour
Fording depth:	c. 1.20 m, 4.0 m with snorkel

An Strv 122 of the Swedish Armed Forces. One can see here the smoke mortar installation and thicker turret roof armour. (Eilert Gezelius/Swedish Armed Forces)

M-84AS

In 2004 with Russian help, Serbia introduced its thoroughly modernized M-84AS (also M-2001) with new compound and reactive armour, new fire-control system and a 1200-hp diesel. The M84-AS has the capability of firing laser-guided Type 9M119 missiles from the cannon and is fitted with the *Soft-Kill Schtora-1* system which intercepts incoming IR- and laser-guided missiles. It is not known however how many of the 212 vehicles of the Serbian M-84 fleet have been equipped in this manner. There are at present no export contracts. The only other user of the M-84 is Bosnia Herzegovina which has a small number of them, exactly how many is not known. Those technical details correspond to the M-84, but the technical details of the M-84AS do not correspond exactly to those of the basic model! The M-84AS weighs 45 tonnes, and its new 1200-hp motor provides a power/weight ratio of 26.7 hp/tonne and over 70 km/hr. Dimensions and armament are otherwise those of the basic M-84 model.

The Serbian M-84AS was developed with Russian help and resembles the T-90. Photograph taken at the "Partner 2009" Armaments Fair in May 2209, Belgrade, Serbia. (Kos93, cc by sa. 3.0)

Olifant

Since 1957 South Africa had obtained 250 *Centurions* Mk 2 and 3 from Great Britain and later other Mk 5s from Jordan and India, all of which had a 20-pounder cannon (83.4 mm). By the mid-1970s a small number of these (35) had been given new motors and transmission (and re- designated Centurion Mk 5A *Semel*). A major upgrading in fighting worth was not begun until 1976, however, when around 300 *Centurions* received engine overhaul, improved chassis, new turret swivel installation, low light level amplifiers and IR searchlights. More or less the old *Centurion* fire-control system was retained and the commander now had a hand-held laser rangefinder. The units received the first *Olifant* Mk 1s in 1978. When the fighting in Angola showed the inferiority of the 83.4 mm cannon to the T54/55, a new gun was installed from 1983 which combined the 105-mm L/7 barrel with the original breech ring of the 20-pounder. Additionally the laser-rangefinder was now intgrated into the gunlayer's optic, the night vision equipment was improved and a new 750-hp diesel with automatic transmission fitted (*Olifant* Mk 1A). From 1991 the *Olifant* Mk 1B was ready, and this was practically a new vehicle. The Mk 1B had new

Type:	Olifant Mk 1B
Manufacturer:	Reumech OMC (later Alvis OMC, today BAE Land Systems)
Battle weight:	58 tonnes
Length:	8600 mm (hull) 10200 mm (with barrel)
Breadth:	3390 mm (with lateral aprons)
Height:	2900 mm (upper side turret)
Motor:	12-cylinder diesel
Efficiency kW/hp:	662/900
Power/weight ratio:	15.52 hp/tonne
Top speed:	58 km/hr (road)
Fuel capacity:	1240 litres
Range:	500 km
Crew:	4
Armament:	1 x 105 mm GT3 L/51 cannon 1 x 7.62 mm coaxial MG 1 x 7.62 mm AA MG 2 x 4 smoke mortars
Armour:	19-152 mm steel armour, schott armour, additional armour from compound material
Fording depth:	c. 1.20 m.

Olifant Mk 1A, the track guards usually fitted are absent here. (South African Army)

During a visit to South Africa by the US Army on 27 March 2011, soldiers and public see over an Olifant Mk 1B. (US Army)

Althouth the Olifant Mk 1B is based on the Centurion, in reality it is a new design and even outwardly bears little resemblance to the British tank. (Vincent Bourguignon)

bogie with torsion bar suspension, a thermal barrel sleeve, longer hull with 900-hp diesel, new transmission, a modern fire-control installation with laser-rangefinder and other changes. The front of the hull and turret were given additional protection of compound material: in this area the tank also received proximity or *schott* armour which gave the turret a completely new profile. Additionally new track aprons were fitted and the hull floor given *schott* armour protection against landmines. A white-light/IR

searchlight was mounted above the cannon. In 2003 Alvis OMC received the contract to modernize 13 Olifant Mk 1B's with improved drive unit, and fit the fire-control system with new optics and thermal imaging sight. This was followed in 2005 by a contract to equip over 13 tanks with modified turret (modular compound armour), a 120-mm smooth bore or 105-mm rifled bore cannon, new fire-control system and stabilized optics (*Olifant* Mk 2). A recovery tank was also built on the *Olifant* basis. At the time of writing the South African Army has over 250 *Olifants*, most of them mothballed for financial reasons.

At the beginning of the 1990s ARMSCOR, Denel and ReuMech introduced the prototype of a tank developed entirely in South Africa, *Tank Technology Demonstrator* (TTD), the compound armour of which gave it the typical squarish look of modern Western battle tanks resembling the *Leopard 2*. The TTD weighed 58 tonnes and was equipped with a 1250-hp diesel, digital fire-control system and a 105-mm cannon (series-produced tanks were to have had a 120-mm smooth bore cannon.) For lack of the means, the development was cancelled.

The Olifant Mk 2 did not proceed beyond the experimental stage and only a few examples were built. (South African Army)

K-1

Since the mid-1970s the South Korean Government had been looking for a modern successor for their Type M47 and M48 tanks. The replacements had to be tailored for the specific requirements of their territory (mountainous terrain, small physical stature of their troops, infrastructure). Because their own industry was not in a position to design such a vehicle, the contract was awarded finally to the US firm Chrysler Defence (today General Dynamics Land Systems) in 1979. The first prototypes (XK1) were completed in 1983 and mass production began in 1985/86. The K1, also known respectively as 88 and ROKIT (Republic of Korea Indigenous Tank), bore some similarities to the M1 *Abrams* which was also Chrysler designed. In common with the M1 the K1 was protected at the front and sides by a USA-produced compound armour of the *Chobham* type and equipped with a 105-mm rifled barrel M68 cannon completed under licence in Korea with thermal barrel sleeve and smoke extractor. Except for the commander's French-made stabilized optic the fire-control and gun-stabilization installations match those of the M1 in many respects. The bogie is specially designed to South Korean requirements,

Type:	K1 (K1A1)
Manufacturer:	Hyundai Rotem
Battle weight:	51,100 kg (53,200 kg)
Length:	7477 mm (hull) 9672 mm (with barrel) (9710 mm)
Breadth:	3594 mm (with lateral aprons)
Height:	2248 mm (upper side turret)
Motor:	MTU MB 871 Ka 501 10-cylinder diesel
Efficiency kW/hp:	883/1200
Power/weight ratio:	23.48 hp/tonne (22.56 hp/tonne)
Top speed:	65 km/hr (road)
Fuel capacity:	n/a
Range:	450 km
Crew:	4
Armament:	1 x 105 mm M68 L/51 cannon (120 mm M256 L/144) 1 x 7.62 mm coaxial MG 1 x 12.7 mm and 1 x 7.62 mm AA MG 2 x 6 smoke mortars
Armour:	steel armour, Chobham compound protection
Fording depth:	c. 1.2 m, 5 m with snorkel

A K1 of 57.Cavalry Batallion/26 Division, South Korean Army at Camp Casey, Gyeonggi-do Province, South Korea awaiting train transport on 24 March 2006. (US Army)

A K1 leaving a US Air Cushion Landing Craft at Pohang Beach, Korea on 26 March 2004 during a joint exercise. (US DoD)

only the central pair of rolling wheels have conventional torsion rods, pairs 1, 2 and 6 have hydropneumatic suspension so that the front or rear of the hull can be inclined to increase the elevation/depression range of the cannon – in mountainous terrain a great advantage. The two prototypes built in the USA were given US diesels (AVCR-1790) and US gearing, but the series tanks received a German drive unit. The MTU MB 871 Ka 501 1200 hp engine is a more compact version of the diesel used by the *Leopard 2*.

In 1996 the first prototype of the improved version K1A1 was introduced, series production of

which began in 1999. The K1A1 has a 120-mm smooth bore M256 cannon (the US version of the Rheinmetall 120-mm L/44 cannon of the *Leopard 2*) and an improved fire-control installation with new thermal imaging unit, new laser-rangefinder and new stabilization system for the cannon. In addition the armour was reinforced with a layer of depleted uranium as in later versions of the M1. This resulted in a weight increase of 2 tonnes or more. Up to 1998, 1027 K1s left the assembly halls of Hyundai Rotem, and from 1999 to 2010 484 tanks K1A1. Additionally a recovery tank was produced in cooperation with MaK (Kiel) and with Vickers a bridgelayer.

From 1999 to 2010 a total of 484 K1A1 improved variants with 120-mm cannon and new turret were completed. (Hyundai Rotem)

K2 Black Panther

The K2 is planned as the successor to and replacement for the K1. Its development began in 1995. The K2 first displayed in public in 2007 can be considered one of the most modern and costly battle tanks in the world, but remains in the prototype stage at the time of writing. Series production was set back several times for difficulties with the motor and transmission. Although the tank was developed under the auspices of the Korean Defence Agency, and around 90% of the components were manufactured in Korea, European firms such as GIAT (today Nexter) and Diehl were also involved. The K2 is fitted with a compound armour of the newest kind at the front of the vehicle.

Additionally ERA elements have been mounted to the sides and turret. Besides laser-, radar-warning and counter-measures systems, the K2 has its own millimeter-frequency radar which warns of approaching projectiles and activates automatically the smoke- and deceptive counter-measures mortars. These not only obscure the tank visually, but also block enemy laser-, IR- and radar beams. The system also calculates from where the projectile was fired so that the trank crew can react against it immediately. It is also planned to install a *Hard-Kill* system in the future. It was originally intended to have a Rheinmetall-built 140 mm smooth bore cannon, but the development of this weapon was discontinued and so a 120-mm smooth bore L/55 gun completed in Korea under licence is to replace it. Ammunition feed for this gun is by automatic loader, similar to that of the *Leclerc*, installed in the rear of the turret thus enabling the number of crew to be reduced to three (driver, gunner and commander). So-called "blow-out" panels are integrated into the upper side of the turret rear and open outwards in the event of ammunition exploding, thus diverting the energy of the detonation away from the confines of the armoured room. The K2 has a digital fire-control installation of the most modern type developed in Korea and includes a laser-rangefinder, crosswind sensor,

Type:	K2 Black Panther
Manufacturer:	Hyundai Rotem
Battle weight:	55 tonnes
Length:	7500 mm (hull) 10800 mm (with barrel)
Breadth:	3600 mm (with lateral aprons)
Height:	2400 mm (upper side turret)
Motor:	MTU MB 883 Ka500 12-cylinder diesel
Efficiency kW/hp:	1103/1500
Power/weight ratio:	27.27 hp/tonne
Top speed:	70 km/hr (road) 50 km/hr (terrain)
Fuel capacity:	n/a
Range:	450 km
Crew:	3
Armament:	1 x 120 mm L/55 cannon 1 x 7.62 mm coaxial MG 1 x 12.7 mm and 1 x 7.62 mm AA MG 2 x 6 smoke mortars and 1 x 8 deceptive-counter-measure mortars
Armour:	steel armour, Chobham compound protection, ERA and NERA
Fording depth:	c. 1.2 m, 5 m with snorkel

thermal imaging unit and an independent rotatable commander's optic. The fire-control is coupled to the radar installation and can exchange data with other tanks similarly equipped into the network. At the design stage great emphasis was laid upon the network centric warfare and C4I capabilities. The tank also has an IFF installation and GPS navigation system. The Korean forces are hoping in future to have a small unmanned wheeled vehicle (XAV) integral to the K2-system for the reconnoitring of dangerous areas. The K2 has hydropenuematic suspension so that any one of its six roller wheels can be used individually. This enables the tank to be inclined to vary the forward or rear ground clearance or be swerved in any direction. Originally the K2 was

The K2 prototypes are also known as XK2.Notice the millimetre-radar system at the turret front and the mortars positioned on the turret roof to launch deceptive counter-measures. (Hyundai Rotem)

The K2 is probably one of the most modern tanks anywhere. Series production was scheduled for the end of 2013. (Hyundai Rotem)sein. (Hyundai Rotem)

to have been equipped with a drive unit developed in Korea but problems of production led to many postponements of the series run. The first 100 series-vehicles are now due to be fitted with MTU MB-883 Ka500 diesels and German transmission and the planned start for the run is the end of 2013.

T-72M4CZ

The T-72 was built under licence in the former Czechoslovakia and made up a good part of its tank fleet. After the country was split into the Czech Republic and Slovakia in 1993, the Czech Government decided that their T-72s should undergo a comprehensive modernization process. This included a new drive unit conceived in Israel (British Perkins 1000-hp diesel and automatic Allison transmission from the United States), an Officine Galileo digital fire-control installation from Italy (also found in the battle tank *Ariete*) with thermal imaging, crosswind sensor, laser-rangefinder and an independent commander's optic positioned on the roof of the turret. The main weapon would be retained but with a muzzle reference system for checking calibration. Additionally there was a German explosion-suppression installation, a Polish warning system and Polish developed reactive armour (DYNA), and an inertial navigation system with integral GPS. Although the Czech Army requirement had been documented at 355 tanks, this number was reduced later to 250. In the 21st century only 33 T-72s have been upgraded to this standard and the future of the programme is uncertain.

Type:	T72M4CZ
Manufacturer:	VOP (conversion)
Battle weight:	48 tonnes
Length:	6950 mm (hull) 9820 mm (with barrel)
Breadth:	3755 mm (with lateral aprons)
Height:	2280 mm (without AA gun), 272o mm (with commander's optic)
Motor:	12-cylinder Perkins CV-12 100 TCA diesel
Efficiency kW/hp:	736/1000
Power/weight ratio:	20.83 hp/tonne
Top speed:	61 km/hr (road)
Fuel capacity:	1200 litres (internal)
Range:	450 km (600 km with 2 x 200 litre supplementary tanks at rear)
Crew:	3
Armament:	1 x 125 mm 2A46M cannon 1 x 7.62 mm coaxial MG 1 x 12.7 mm AA MG
Armour:	steel armour, compound protection, ERA

The T-72M4CZ is a variant of the T-72 comprehensively upgraded for battleworthiness, but the future of the programme is uncertain. (VOP.cz)

M60T

This M-60 version with improved armour and the 120-mm smooth bore MG253 gun of the *Merkava IV* is the result of experience gained from the *Magach* series developed by IMI (Israel Military Industries). Up until then the only client was the Turkish military. The Turkish version (*Sabra* Mk II or M60T) has some differences from the original design. The M19 commander's cupola with 12.7-mm MG M85 is retained with thermal imaging unit added. The tank also received a 1000-hp MTU diesel and RENK transmission built in Turkey under licence, and reactive armour in the front area. The combat readiness upgrade included the modernization of the entire electrical system, an electrical turret-swivel and weapons stabilization installation, fire extinguishing- and explosion-suppressor unit, a new fire-control system and changes to the bogie. The contract between IMI and Turkey was signed in 2002 and the first prototypes emerged for trials in 2005. Between 2007 and 2009 the Turkish Army converted 170 of their M60s to M60T. Apart from the armour, practically all components are made in Turkey under licence. Accordingly the Turkish Army is planning in future to convert more M60s to this fighting level but now without Israeli help.

Type:	M60T
Manufacturer:	Turkish Army workshops/IMI
Battle weight:	59 tonnes
Length:	6950 mm (hull) 9400 mm (with barrel)
Breadth:	3630 mm (with lateral aprons)
Height:	3270 mm (upper side turret)
Motor:	MTU 881 Ka 501 12-cylinder diesel
Efficiency kW/hp:	735/1000
Power/weight ratio:	16.95 hp/tonne
Top speed:	55 km/hr (road)
Fuel capacity:	n/a
Range:	450 km
Crew:	4
Armament:	1 x 120 mm MG253 L/44 cannon 1 x 7.62 mm coaxial MG 1 x 12.7 mm AA MG 1 x 60-mm mortar 2 x 4 smoke mortars
Armour:	max 254 mm steel armour with modular compound protection and ERA
Fording depth:	1.22 m, 4.5 m with snorkel

The M60T is based on the Israeli Magach developments but with major differences, and most are built in Turkey. (Turkish Defence Ministry)

Altay

The *Altay* is based on the Korean K2 with substantial modifications. In 2005 the Turkish Government pressed for a domestic-built battle tank, and in 2007 cooperation with Hyundai Rotem was agreed. An initial mock-up was presented in 2011, and the following year testing of the first prototypes began. Turkey plans to have 1000 *Altay* (produced in four batches each of 250 vehicles). The main difference from the K2 are a longer hull with seven instead of six roller wheels, a new turret, the rejection of an automatic loader for the cannon, and improved protection. All these changes make the *Altay* at around 66 tonnes much heavier than the K2. Numerous components including the armour, fire-control system and electronics are Turkish home developments, the 120-mm L/55 Rheinmetal gun was made under licence. A remote weapons station with 12.7-mm MG is to be built into the turret roof. No reliable information is forthcoming as to whether an ECM-, *Soft-* or *Hard-Kill Systems* are to be fitted. The first two batches (500 tanks) are to receive the 1500-hp MTU MB-883 diesel, afterwards Turkey hopes to have the home-produced 1800-hp diesel available.

Type:	Altay
Manufacturer:	Otokar
Battle weight:	66 tonnes
Length:	n/a
Breadth:	n/a
Height:	n/a
Motor:	MTU MB 883 Ka500 12-cylinder diesel
Efficiency kW/hp:	1103/1500
Power/weight ratio:	22.72 hp/tonne
Top speed:	70 km/hr (road) 50 km/hr (terrain)
Fuel capacity:	n/a
Range:	400-500 km
Crew:	4
Armament:	1 x 120 mm L/55 cannon 1 x 7.62 mm coaxial MG 1 x 12.7 mm AA MG 2 x 8 smoke mortars
Armour:	steel armour, compound protection, ERA and NERA
Fording depth:	1.2 m, 4.1 m with snorkel

The Altay is the first battle tank to be developed and built in Turkey. Series production is expected to continue until 2015. (OTOKAR)

T-64

The first T-64 models were produced in 1964 and but nevertheless are mentioned here for their very progressive and futuristic concept. The T-64 was the first tank anywhere to be series-produced with compound protection and automatic loading for the main weapon. The Red Army leadership had recognized by the end of the 1950s that the development potential of the T-54/55/62 range was exhausted and therefore ordered a completely new design. The Kharkov Design Office came up with "Project 432" which entered series production in 1964 as the T-64. Although still fitted initially with the 115-mm gun of the T-62, the design was otherwise revolutionary. In order to remain within the weight and dimensional limits of the earlier range despite the substantial change in performance, numerous innovations became necessary. Therefore the T-64 was given a new bogie with six small, light roller wheels hung on torsion bars. The newly designed and very compact diesel worked on the opposed piston principle in order to obtain maximum efficiency. To

Type:	T-64A
Manufacturer:	Tank Works Kharkov
Battle weight:	38 tonnes
Length:	7400 mm (hull) 9250 mm (with barrel)
Breadth:	3415 mm
Height:	2170 mm (without AA gun)
Motor:	5-cylinder opposed piston diesel 5TDF
Efficiency kW/hp:	515/700
Power/weight ratio:	18.42 hp/tonne
Top speed:	70 km/hr (road)
Fuel capacity:	1270 litres (internal)
Range:	500 km (700 km with 2 x 200 litres supplementary tanks at rear
Crew:	3
Armament:	1 x 125 mm 2A46 cannon 1 x 7.62 mm coaxial MG 1 x 12.7 mm AA MG
Armour:	steel armour, compound protection
Fording depth:	1.8 m, 5 m with snorkel

An early T-84 (still fitted with the 115-mm cannon) fording a river. (US Army)

This T-64A is seen in the tank collection at the Suvorov Military Academy, Moscow. (Vitaly V. Kuzmin)

keep the dimensions as small as possible the fourth crewman, the gunloader, was dispensed with and his job taken over by an automatic loader, a carousel-style magazine on the turret floor with 28 rounds and propellant charges delivered forward mechanically to the fully stabilized cannon. In the turret the gunlayer sat on the left, the commander on the right, the driver had a seat placed centrally in the hull forward. In order to maximize the protection, particularly against incoming hollow-charge missiles, compound armour was built into the front areas of hull and turret, a novelty in tank construction. The fire-control unit was thoroughly progressive and had an optical rangefinder aboard a Soviet tank for the first time. The vehicle could make smoke by spraying diesel fuel into the exhaust system. Although production was in hand in 1964, the basic model of the T-64 did not begin to enter Red Army service officially until the end of 1966 on account of continuing problems with the automatic loader, the wheels and tracks and

particularly the engine and radiator. Therefore the modest total for Soviet needs of only 1032 T-64s had come off the production line by 1968.

Completion of the T-64A began in 1969, this model having a different radiator and revised automatic loader. A 125-mm 2A26 cannon with modified stabilization, new optics, improved IR searchlight, increased compound armour and folding side aprons had also been mounted. The command version T-64AK had additional radio and navigation equipment. In the course of production and operationally the A/AK version modifications were carried out partly at the works, and partly by the troops themselves. Thus from 1972 amongst other additions a better fire-control system and an anti-aircraft MG were installed, the later capable of being aimed and fired from within the tank, while in 1975 a revised 125-mm cannon (2A46) with thermal barrel sleeve, modified automatic loader, new stabilizing system and new night vision equipment followed.

The motor was adapted to the Vielstoff capability (see Glossary). From 1981 the folding side aprons were replaced by rubber track guards, while a laser-rangefinder and smoke mortars were fitted. From 1983 some T-64As were given a more efficient motor (T-64AM or AKM), and from the mid-1970s numerous T-64s were brought up to the standard of the T-64A and re-designated T-64R.

The command version of the T-64A was designated T-64AK. This example photographed in June 2008 is in the T-34 Museum near Moscow. (Vitaly V.Kuzmin)

T-64B

The T-64B version was built from 1975. It had a newly-designed turret with increased compound armour, a modified automatic loader and a new fire-control system with integrated laser-rangefinder. This Type also had the operational capability for its 125-mm smooth bore cannon to fire the radio-controlled missile 9K112 Kobra (NATO designation AT-8 *Songster*) effective against battle tanks and helicopters at up to four miles' range. Tanks without this capability were designated T-64BK. From 1981 as with the A version smoke mortars were fitted and an improved version of the 125-mm cannon. In 1985 the variant T-64BW appeared (analogous to it B1W and BWK) which had a total of 115 ERA *Kontakt*-1 blocks on the hull and turret front, and sides. The T-64BW had a coating of Kevlar and anti-radiation protection on the inside of the turret. This Type also had an improved 125-mm 2A46 cannon. A series of tanks of this variant were later fitted with Type 6TD 850-hp diesels and re-designated T-64BWM, B1WM and BKM. Production ended in 1987. In all, around 8,000 T-64 of all types were manufactured over a period of twenty years, measured by Soviet standards relatively few.

Type:	T-64B
Manufacturer:	Tank Works Kharkov
Battle weight:	40,400 kg BW's 42,500 kg
Length:	7400 mm (hull) 9240 mm (with barrel)
Breadth:	3460 mm BW's 3600 mm
Height:	2200 mm (less AA weapon)
Motor:	5-cylinder opposed piston 5TDF
Efficiency kW/hp:	515/700
Power/weight ratio:	17.2 hp/tonne (BV 16.5 hp/tonne)
Top speed:	70 km/hr (road), BV 656 km/hr
Fuel capacity:	1270 litres internal
Range:	500 km (700 km with 2 x 200 litre supplementary tanks at rear)
Crew:	3
Armament:	1 x 125 mm 2A46 cannon 1 x 7.62 mm coaxial MG 1 x 12.7 mm AA MG
Armour:	steel armour, compound protection (20-450 mm), BW's with reactive armour
Fording depth:	1.8 m, 5 m with snorkel

A T-64BW of the Forces of Transnistria (as at 2016 the unrecognized Republic of Pridnestrovian Moldavia also known as Transdniester) which has a small number of these tanks. Photograph taken at capital town Tiraspol, 2 September 2010. (Spender, cc by sa 3.0)

The T-64 had been envisaged originally as the standard battle tank of the Red Army and was not to have been built only at Kharkov, but at other large tank factories throughout the USSR. For its time the tank was very progressive and went to the limits of what was possible in the Soviet Union. Precisely for this reason the T-64 was not properly tried and tested and was therefore unreliable, and this did not change until the T-64B. Besides their chronic susceptibility to breakdowns, especially the motors, the high price was the great shortcoming of the Type – it cost almost twice as much as a T-72. The T-64 was therefore never exported, and not even used operationally by Warsaw Pact forces. Only Red Army units in the Soviet Union itself, the Eastern Zone of Germany and Hungary drove it. After the collapse of the Soviet Union most T-64s remained in Russian or

A T-64B1 with snorkel.

Ukrainian hands, although about 100 were taken by Uzbekistan. Many T-64s are kept meanwhile in reserve or in store in Russia and the Ukraine, or have been scrapped. In mid-2009 it was reported additionally that Russia had passed about 100 T-64BWs to Azerbaijan.

The T-64B1 version seen here was not able to fire the AT-8 Songster missile for reasons of cost.

T-72

The T-64, developed and built at Kharkov, was intended to be the standard battle tank of the Red Army built at all USSR tank factories. In 1967 the preparations for mass production were called off and the design office at Nishni Tagil given the job of developing a version capable of series production in time of war. The main weakness of the early T-64 was the 5TDF two-stroke diesel. Because this engine was very small, the hull had now to be redesigned to take a much larger installation. A four-stroke diesel (a further development of the T-34/44/54/55/62 series) was 80-hp more efficient than the 5-TDF but overburdened the T-64 bogie, already very prone to breakdown, and this called for larger rolling wheels. By reason of the numerous necessary changes, in May 1970 Nishni Tagil finally received permission to develop its own battle tank. The end result was a completely new Type, the T-72. After intensive trials of the prototypes and pre-series examples between 1970 and 1973, at the beginning of 1974 mass production began at the Uralwaggons Works at Nishni Tagil.

Type:	T-72
Manufacturer:	Tank Works Nishni Tagil (development)
Battle weight:	41 tonnes
Length:	6950 mm (hull) 9533 mm (with barrel)
Breadth:	3460 mm (without lateral aprons)
Height:	2230 mm (without AA gun)
Motor:	W-46 12-cylinder diesel
Efficiency kW/hp:	574/780
Power/weight ratio:	19.02 hp/tonne
Top speed:	60 km/hr (road)
Fuel capacity:	1200 litres (internal)
Range:	500 km (700 km with 2 x 200 litre supplementary tanks at rear)
Crew:	3
Armament:	1 x 125 mm 2A26 cannon 1 x 7.62 mm coaxial MG 1 x 12.7 mm AA MG
Armour:	steel armour, compound protection
Fording depth:	1.8 m, 5 m with snorkel

This early T-72 once saw service with the Czechoslovak People's Army but is seen here in the Worthington Tank Museum at Ontario, Canada. The track guards were not added until the 1980s. (Balcer, cc by sa 3.0)

The basic version of the T-72 (recognizable by the viewing ports of the optical rangefinder at the upper sides of the turret) at a parade in Moscow at the end of the 1970s. (US DoD9)

The T-72 resembled the T-64 not only in its concept and dimensions, but had the same armament, a fully stabilized 125-mm smooth bore B2A26 cannon with automatic loader. This differed from the T-64 in that shell and propellant charge were separated into two working processes, and at first the magazine held only 22 rounds. The original T-72 was equipped with optical rangefinder and IR searchlights for night actions. The driver was seated centrally forward in the hull and the relatively small, rather rounded cast steel turret was at the middle of the vehicle: in the turret the commander sat at the right and the gunlayer at the left. Although the hull front of even the first models had *schott* armour with artificial filling, the turret was initially only protected by steel armour. In common with all Soviet battle tanks, supplementary fuel tanks could be fitted at the rear, and mine clearance equipment or a bulldozer-type shield at the front. The T-72 could also make smoke by spraying diesel fuel into the exhaust system.

The T-72 was subject to continuous improvments during the course of production. As a result there are numerous versions with a multitude of sub-variants and later additions, and special models for export. These latter would frequently have bits and pieces "sliced off", for example the armour might be weaker, there would be no NBC protection or some other kind of fire-control system installed. The Type was also built under licence in Poland, Czechoslovakia, India, the former Yugoslavia, Iran and Iraq. Occasionally the designations overlapped or contradicted each other. A complete list of all sub-variants would not be possible here.

Many versions also had their own command tank with additional radio and navigation equipment (indicated by a "K", therefore T-72K, T-72AK etc.), and variants with reactive additional armour (often but not always, might receive the suffix "W", such as T-72AW, T-72BW etc.)

T-72A

The T-72A appeared in 1979 and had an improved gun (model 2A46) and modernized fire-control system with laser-rangefinder. The IR searchlight was now placed at the right side of the gun. Beside a range of minor alterations this version was distinguished primarily by its improved protection. In place of the folding side aprons rubber track guards were fitted as a permanent feature. The turret front and roof were now protected by a voluptuous compound armour known as *Dolly Parton* to the Americans. Later another 16-mm armour plate was added to the hull front, smoke mortars were installed on the turret and internally an anti-radiation shielding. The "A" model of the version known as T-72M was built in the Soviet Union, Czechoslovakia and Poland for export with less armour and a less efficient fire-control system. The M1 version on the other hand had more armour and 12 smoke mortars at the front of the turret.

Type:	T-72A
Manufacturer:	Tank Works Nishni Tagil (development)
Battle weight:	41,500 kg
Length:	6950 mm (hull) 9533 mm (with barrel)
Breadth:	3460 mm, 3590 mm (with lateral aprons)
Height:	2230 mm (less AA gun)
Motor:	W-46 12-cylinder diesel
Efficiency kW/hp:	574/780
Power/weight ratio:	18.8 hp/tonne
Top speed:	68 km/hr (road)
Fuel capacity:	1200 litres (internal)
Range:	450 km (600 km with 2 x 200 litre supplementary tanks at rear)
Crew:	3
Armament:	1 x 125 mm 2A46 cannon 1 x 7.62 mm coaxial MG 1 x 12.7 mm AA MG 1 x 8 smoke mortars
Armour:	steel armour, compound protection
Fording depth:	1.8 m, 5 m with snorkel

T-72A's at the parade in Moscow in 1983 to celebrate the October Revolution. (Thomas Hedden, PD)

T-72B

The T-72B version was introduced in 1985 with reinforced compound armour, an improved fire-control installation, an 840 hp engine and a Type 2A46M cannon able to fire the laser-guided anti-tank missile 9M119 Svir (NATO designation AT-11 *Sniper*). Tanks lacking this capability (and the T-72A optics) are classified as T-72B1. The T-72BA or BW has more than 227 ERA *Kontakt*-1 type blocks attached to the turret, hull front and track guards, while the T-72B export version, the variant T-72S, has only 155 and a simplified NBC protection and no anti-radiation coating. Type BM which appeared in 1989 has improved compound armour now stretching along the turret sides, and *Kontakt*-5 type reactive armour had also been added. In the model built from 1990 the fire-control installation and sometimes a more powerful motor (1000 hp) were fitted. In the West these two versions are often classified as T-72BM while in the USSR/Russia the designation is T-72B *obr.1989* and *1990* respectively. The further development of the T-72 then led to the T-90. The T-72 served as the basis for recovery tanks (BREM), pioneer tanks (IRM), bridgelayers (MTU), rocket-launchers (TOS-1 and even a heavy infantry battle tank (BMPT) to mention just a few. The T-72 series is amongst the most-built tanks of all time (in the USSR/Russia it is reported that more than 25,000 of them have been

Type:	T-72B
Manufacturer:	Tank Works Nishni Tagil (development)
Battle weight:	46,500 kg
Length:	6950 mm (hull) 9533 mm (with barrel)
Breadth:	3460 mm, 3590 mm (with lateral aprons)
Height:	2280 mm (without AA gun)
Motor:	V-46 12-cylinder diesel
Efficiency kW/hp:	618/840
Power/weight ratio:	18.06 hp/tonne
Top speed:	60 km/hr (road)
Fuel capacity:	1200 litres (internal)
Range:	450 km (600 km with 2 x 200 litre supplementary tanks at rear)
Crew:	3
Armament:	1 x 125 mm 2A46M cannon 1 x 7.62 mm coaxial MG 1 x 12.7 mm AA MG 1 x 8 smoke mortars
Armour:	steel armour, compound protection era
Fording depth:	1.8 m, 5 m with snorkel

manufactured, not to mention those built under licence elsewhere) and being exported in large numbers have seen action in many conflicts

A T-72B1 (T-72B lacking capability to fire the anti-tank AT-11 missile) of the Georgian Army. Note the numerous blocks of the additional reactive armour. Vaziani, Georgia, September 2005. (USMC)

T-72B (with reactive armour) of the Russian forces during the war in Georgia in August 2008. The circumstance that, as here, the T-72 was used by both sides at the fighting front occurred on several occasions previously such as in the 1991 Gulf War, the wars in Yugoslavia or the Libyan civil war of 2011, to mention only a few. (Novosti Press)

worldwide, amongst others the Iran-Iraq War (1980-1988), the two Gulf Wars (1990/91 and 2003), the war in Lebanon in 1982, the conflicts in the 1990s in the former Yugoslavia, in Libya in 2011 and since 2011 in the Syrian civil war.

The T-72 did not win for itself any specially good reputation though the criticism was not down to its design, but largely to poorly trained and motivated crews (e.g. 1990/91 in Iraq), to obsolete ammunition and sub-standard export models. The T-72 is a relatively small tank offering not much of a target, but has little room to move inside it. The T-72 automatic

loader is not always reliable (especially on the earlier versions): if it fails, manual loading is laborious and time-consuming. Additionally storing the ammunition in a carousel-magazine on the turret floor has its dangers, for if the tank sets off a landmine or receives a shell hit the whole turret can be blasted off. A hit which penetrates the turret room is usually catstrophic in effect even on Western tanks of course. In comparison to modern tanks the T-72 is obviously becoming obsolete but for many national buyers it remains as attractive as ever for its robust, financially economic design, relatively low cost of

maintenance and simplicity in use. In 2012 the Type was still in commission in 30 States and to all intents and purposes will long remain so. Factories in numerous countries therefore offer a combat-worthiness upgrading programme for the T-72.

Numerous firms offer a combat-worthiness upgrading programme for the T-72, such as KMDB at Kharkov in the Ukraine. Their programme includes comprehensive modifications to the fire-control unit and its optics, also passive and reactive additional armour, a Ukrainian 125-mm KBA1 cannon and a new 1000-hp or 1200-hp diesel. Until now its only client has been Algeria, which has around 500 T-72s.

T-80

The T-80 is based on the T-64 and was the first tank anywhere to have gas-turbine drive only. It was planned that it would replace the T-64 and T-72 as the standard tank of the Red Army. The first trials by the Leningrad Tank Works with turbine-driven T-64s took place at the end of the 1960s. The enhanced performance of the new engine made an extensive redesign necessary, especially the undercarriage. Diverse problems, particularly with the turbine (reliability, high consumption) held back the development for years and series production did not begin until 1976. By the mid-1990s, around 5,400 T-80s had been completed. During the course of this time primarily the armour protection and fire-control unit were being continually improved. For lack of

space the numerous versions of the T-80 cannot be presented here, only the most important models: command-vehicle variants are identified by the suffix "K" and have additional communications and navigational equipment. Variants with ERA were given the suffix "W" (e.g. T-80BW), other versions, e.g. without guided weapon capability, by a "1" (e.g. T-80B1). The main difference between the T-80 and T-64A was the equipping of the former with a 1000-hp gas turbine and new bogie with six large rolling wheels and torsion bar suspension. Armament, protection and automatic loader were identical, even the T-80 turret was based on that of the T-64A with optical rangefinder and IR searchlight. At the time of its introduction, in its technology the T-80 had already fallen behind the T-64B and was therefore only built in very small numbers (around 200) subsequently.

A T-80B in the St. Petersburg Artillery Musuem photogrpahed in May 2007. In contrast to the T-72 notice the smaller rolling wheels with the typical gaps between the second and third, and fourth and fifth wheels. (PD)

T-80B

The T-80B was produced from 1978 and had a revised turret, more modern fire-control system with laser-rangefinder and modified automatic loader. This version was able to fire the radio-guided 9K112 *Kobra* missile (NATO designation AT-8 *Songster*). It also had a very thick armour in the front area. From 1980 an 1100-hp turbine was added, and from 1985 the model received reactive armour (T-80BW). The versions "B" and "BW" were the most-built variants, around 4,500 T-80s with this specification were completed. The T-80A built from 1982 had a newly developed compound armour, a 1200-hp turbine, modified fire-control unit and a revised 125-mm cannon able to fire the laser-guided 9M119M *Refleks* missile (AT-11 Sniper).

A T-80BW with Kontakt-5 reactive armour to hull and turret. (Vitaly V. Kuzmin)

T-80U

Only a few dozen T-80A's were built before the T-80U entered series production in 1986. This variant received improved compound armour, an 1100-hp turbine, a more efficient fire-control system and a new turret. Turret and hull front are protected by ERA *Kontakt*-5 blocks. The IR searchlight on the commander's cupola was replaced by a low light level amplifier in its optic. Supplementary to the rubber aprons customary to the T-80, another armour element was added above the leading three roller wheels. An auxiliary unit (APU) enables the thirsty gas-turbine to be turned off while stationary and supplies enough energy to keep all systems of the tank turning over meanwhile. A 1250-hp turbine was installed in 1990. Later models of the T-80U also received the *Soft-Kill-System Schtora*-1 consisting of an IR-disruptive device, laser warning system with four laser receivers as well as a smoke mortar unit and *Agava* thermal imagining unit. *Schtora*-1 reacts automatically and disrupts the flight control system of anti-tank missiles, enshrouds the tank in smoke and alerts the crew to the danger.

Information regarding the diesel version T-80UD follows in the "Ukraine" section ahead.

T-80B and T-80U were the most efficient and modern of the Soviet battle tanks but a T-80U cost

Type:	T-80B/T-80U
Manufacturer:	Tank Works Leningrad and Omsk
Battle weight:	42,500 kg/46,000 kg
Length:	7400/7000 mm (hull) 9900/9654 mm (with barrel)
Breadth:	3400/3603 mm (with lateral aprons)
Height:	2202/2202 mm (without AA gun)
Motor:	SG-1000/GTD-1250 gas turbine
Efficiency kW/hp:	736/1000 and 919/1250 respectively
Power/weight ratio:	25.9 hp/tonne and 27.2 hp/tonne respectively
Top speed:	70 km/hr (road)
Fuel capacity:	1840 litres (1100 litres internally + 740 litres external on the track covers.
Range:	330 km (450 km with supplementary tanks)
Crew:	3
Armament:	1 x 125 mm 2A46-2/2A46M-1M cannon 1 x 7.62 mm coaxial MG 1 x 12.7 mm AA MG
Armour:	steel armour, compound protection, T-80BW and U with ERA
Fording depth:	1.8 m, 5 m with snorkel

A T-80U of 4.Independent Brigade at speed. Naro-Fominsk near Moscow, October 2011. (Vitaly V. Kuzmin)

Another T-80U of 4.Independent Brigade. Notice the central turbine exhaust outlet at the rear of the hull and the snorkel at the rear of the turret. Naro-Fominsk near Moscow, October 2011. (Vitaly V. Kuzmin)

three times as much as a T-72B. The gas-turbine provided the T-80 with astounding mobility but came with many disadvantages. It was not only more expensive than the diesel to purchase and maintain (servicing and fuel consumption), but it also generated a stronger heat signature which made the tank visible to thermal imaging instruments at a greater distance. The fact that the T-80 did not become the standard Red Army battle tank, and that the Russian Federation abandoned its production in the mid-1990s, was due mainly to the costs of procurement and maintenance.

The T-80 was only involved on the fringes of fighting especially during conflicts after the collapse of the Soviet Union. The losses (particularly during the first wars in Chechen) were caused less by the deficiencies of the tank than by poor crew training and catastrophic operational errors. Nevertheless, there were instances of turrets being blasted off after

rounds penetrated the armour of the battle room and setting afire the propellant in the magazine on the turret floor.

The T-80 was not exported by the USSR: it was only received by other States after 1991. T-80 then belonged amongst the successors to the Soviet Union (e.g. Ukraine, White Russia, Uzbekistan, Armenia). Export clients were Cyprus (82), China (50), Egypt (34) and Yemen (31). South Korea received a number of T-80Us to indemnify Russian debts carried forward from the Soviet era. These tanks are used in South Korea to impress a potential enemy. Great Britain and the USA also acquired some T-80s for technical investigation in the chaos which followed the dissolution of the USSR. T-80 chassis elements were employed in diverse Soviet tracked vehicles, but the BREM-80 recovery tank and MTU-80 bridgelayer were the only pure offshoots of the T-80.

The T-80U has astounding mobility thanks to its 1250-hp gas turbine. (Vitaly V. Kuzmin)

In 1993 the Swedish Army tested two T-80U's, but finally decided instead for the Leopard 2. (Sven ake Haglund/ Swedish Armed Forces)

Attempts by Russian industry to revive interest in the T-80 came to nought. Neither the prototypes T-80UM-1 Bars and UM, nor a series of experimental vehicles (*Black Eagle*) based on the lengthened T-80 hull with seven roller wheels and ammunition magazine in the rear found any success.

T-90

The T-90 is basically a comprehensively modernized T-72B and was developed in 1990 in Nishni Tagil, the first prototypes being produced in 1993. The T-90 has elements of the T-80U. The hull is practically identical with that of the T-72BW and is likewise protected at the front by *Kontakt*-5 reactive armour. The turret was modified and received reinforced compound armour and *Kontakt*-5 reactive-armour blocks. The *Soft-Kill-System Schtora*-1, which disrupts the guidance system of IR- and laser-guided anti-tank missiles, is also conspicuous. The fire-control installation is a revised version of that system also found in the T-80U. The first T-90s were also fitted with low light level enhancers, later models had an *Agava* thermal imaging unit. The commander's cupola and its optics originate from the T-80U and enable the commander to search for targets, relay the information to the gunner or take on an enemy himself. The commander can lay and fire the 12.7-mm AA gun himself from inside the turret. The main gun is as before a 125-mm smooth bore 2A46 cannon receiving its ammunition from an automatic loader on the turret floor. From the cannonn the T-90 can fire laser-guided missiles (AT-11 *Sniper*) effective against tanks at 4000 metres and

Type:	T-90/T-90A
Manufacturer:	Uralwagonsawod
Battle weight:	46,500 kg/47,500 kg
Length:	6860 mm (hull) 9530 mm (with barrel)
Breadth:	3780 mm (with lateral aprons)
Height:	2260 mm (without AA gun)
Motor:	W-84MS or W-92 12-cylinder diesel
Efficiency kW/hp:	618/840 or 736/1000
Power/weight ratio:	18.06 hp/tonne, 21.05 hp/tonne
Top speed:	60 km/hr (road)
Fuel capacity:	1200 litres
Range:	550 km (7000 km with 2 x 200 litre supplementary tanks at rear)
Crew:	3
Armament:	1 x 125 mm 2A46 cannon 1 x 7.62 mm coaxial MG 1 x 12.7 mm AA MG 2 x 6 smoke mortars
Armour:	steel armour, compound and reactive protection
Fording depth:	1.8 m, 5 m with snorkel

As this side profile of a T-90 shows (photograh taken during the Engineering Technologies Armaments Fair 2010), the relationship to the T-72 in unmistakeable. Moscow, June 2010. (Vitaly V. Kuzmin)

A major user of the T-90 is India, which acquired 620 T-90S and SK from Russia and is planning to build a thousand more under licence. In India the Type is called Bhishma. Indian T-90s hav no Schtora-1 Soft-Kill-System. (Indian Defence Ministry)

low-flying aerial targets at 5000 metres. The engine unit comes from the T-72 (W-84 with 840 hp) providing a comparatively modest mobility. Below the nose of the hull, as in the T-72/T-80 is an excavator blade which can be used to dig in partially. Additionally electro-magnetic or conventional mine clearance systems can be coupled up.

Since series production began in 1994 many variants have made their appearance, but only the most important can be mentioned here for limitations of space. Command versions are given the suffix "K" as in Soviet/Russian tank building practice. The export version T-90S (French thermal imaging unit, 1000-hp diesel and other minor changes) was purchased by Algeria (305) and India (620): India is planning to build at least another thousand T-90s under licence. In 1999 the T-90A appeared with a new, welded turret fitted with stronger compound and reactive armour and driven by a Type W-92 1000-hp diesel.

Of the T-90M introduced in 2009 there is until now only one prototype. It characteristics are amongst other things a new French thermal imagining unit, improved bogie, a 1250-hp diesel and better compound and new *Relikt* ERA protection. In 2011 Uralwagonsawod introduced a programme to upgrade the T-90A (T-90AM). New modular additional armour made a substantial changed to the outer shape. The package includes *Relikt* reactive armour (also added to the new track guards) and cage protection at the hull and turret rear. An 1130-hp diesel with new transmission was also installed, new commander-optics with thermal imaging, a GLONASS satellite navigation systm, a *Schtora*-2 system, a Type 2A82 125-mm cannon and remote 7.62mm weapons station on the turret roof. The 18 rounds of

ammunition are not now kept in a carousel magazine on the turret floor but in a special shell holder at the turret rear so as to offer better protection to the crew against explosions of propellant.

The variants T-90ME and T-90MS are the export versions of the T-90M and T-90AM.

From the mid-1990s until 2005 the Russian Army acquired very few T-90s on the grounds of expense, and by 2012 they had bought around 600 T-90s, 10% of them version T-90A, however the conversion of several hundred old T-72s and the purchase of new T-90s is planned. Turkmenistan has a few dozen T-90s in running order.

The T-90 is probably not as effcient as a Western battle tank, but has proven reliability and systems and is favourable in price. Its main drawback is its relatively weak 840-hp diesel and the dangerous practice of storing propellant in the crew space. On

A T-90A on the way to the general rehearsal for the parade celebrating the 65th anniversary of victory in "The Great War of the Fatherland" (9 May 1945), Moscow 3 May 2010. (Vitaly V. Kuzmin)

T.90A's demonstrating their ability during the Engineering Technologies Armaments Fair 2012. Left and right of the cannon are the IR elements of the Schtora-Soft-Kill System. Moscow, June 2012. (Vitaly V. Kuzmin)

the other hand the *Kontakt*-5 reactive armour and *Schtora Soft-Kill-System* provide very strong protection. Over the next few years the T-90 will form the backbone of the Russian main battle-tank fleet after the possible successors (e.g. T-95) failed to pass the planning stage and no strong contender came into sight. The Russian forces are said to be planning to develop a universal platform known as T-99 *Armatta* which would be the basis for new battle-, infantry-carrier and pioneer-tanks and SP guns. No details are known as yet.

The newest variant of the T-90 is the T-90MS version with new turret rear and motor. Engineering Technologies 2012, Moscow, June 2012. (Vitaly V. Kuzmin)

T-64BM2 Bulat

After the dissolution of the USSR in 1991, the armed forces of the Ukraine "inherited" around 2,400 T-64s. In 1995 KMDB (Kharkiv Morozov Machine Building, the successor to the Soviet Tank Works Kharkov) began the development of a tank of improved combat ability, the version T-64BM2 Bulat, based on the T-64B and introduced publicly in 1999. The Bulat has a more efficient motor (either a 5TDF with 850-hp or a 6TD-1 with 1000-hp): the original cannon was replaced by the KBA3, a 125-mm smooth-bore version of the 2A46 manufactured in the Ukraine and coupled to an automatic loader of the Type used in the T-80UD. The turret front, hull front and side aprons received reactive Kontakt-5 additional armour, the bogie being reinforced to compensate for the extra four tonnes in weight. According to the manufacturer the new digital fire-control system is superior to that of the T-80UD and as an option can take a Ukrainian thermal imaging unit. It is believed that around 100 T-64s have been upgraded to this standard. The T-64U further upgraded version with improved fire-control installation has not emerged so far from the prototype stage.

Type:	T-64BM2 Bulat
Manufacturer:	KMDB
Battle weight:	45 tonnes
Length:	7400 mm (hull) 9240 mm (with barrel)
Breadth:	3600 mm
Height:	2200 mm (without AA MG)
Motor:	5-/6-cylinder opposed piston diesel 5TDFM/6TD-1
Efficiency kW/hp:	625/850 or 735/1000
Power/weight ratio:	18.89 hp/tonne or 22.2 hp/tonne
Top speed:	70 km/hr (road)
Fuel capacity:	1270 litres (internal)
Range:	500 km (700 km with 2 x 200 litre additional tanks at rear)
Crew:	3
Armament:	1 x 125 mm 2A46 cannon 1 x 7.62 mm coaxial MG 1 x 12.7 mm AA MG
Armour:	steel armour, compound and reactive protection
Fording depth:	1.8 m, 5 m with snorkel

A T-64BM2 Bulat of the Ukrainian armed forces. (KMDB)

T-80UD

The main problem of the T-70 was procurement and maintenance of the expensive gas-turbine, for which reason diverse diesel prototypes were sought from 1979. The T-80UD was only built at Kharkov, however, and haltingly. Before the collapse of the Soviet Union only about 500 of them were produced of which in 1991 some 350 partly completed vehicles had been abandoned in a tank park. After the collapse, the factory at Kharkov was retained , but since the new Ukraine was not in a position to build new tanks, the KMDB decided to offer what it had for export. In 1993 after being shown to a Pakistani delegation, two examples were given trials in Pakistan in 1995, and the following year Pakistan announced its interest in buying 320 T-80UD's. 145 of these tanks came from Ukraine Army stocks or the KMDB park, 175 were new constructions with some differences from the original design, e.g. new turrets. Because a number of T-80UD components were of Russian origin (e.g. the cannon and cast steel turret), these were no longer available to the Ukraine. KMDB had therefore designed a new, welded turret and developed its own variant (KBA3) of the 125-mm smooth bore 2A46 cannon. The further development led to the T-84.

Type:	T-80UD
Manufacturer:	Tank Works Kharkov, today KMDB
Battle weight:	46 tonnes
Length:	7085 mm (hull) 9720 mm (with barrel)
Breadth:	3560 mm (with lateral aprons)
Height:	2740 mm (with AA gun)
Motor:	6-cylinder two stroke 6TD-1 diesel
Efficiency kW/hp:	736/1000
Power/weight ratio:	21.74 hp/tonne
Top speed:	65 km/hr (road)
Fuel capacity:	n/a
Range:	580 km
Crew:	3
Armament:	1 x 125 mm KBA3 cannon 1 x 7.62 mm coaxial MG 1 x 12.7 mm AA MG
Armour:	steel armour, compound and ERA protection
Fording depth:	1.8 m, 5 m with snorkel

A T80UD of the Pakistani armoured corps. The Russian T-80UD's are being decommissioned since 2011. The hulls are sent for scrap and the turrets transferred to T-80BW hulls. (Vincent Bourguignon)

T-84

The T-84 is a further development of the T-80UD and differs from it principally by a new, welded turret, a 1200-hp diesel, new electronics and the use of numerous purely Ukrainian designed and manufactured components. After the first protoypes had been exhibited in 1994, the type entered Ukrainian Army service in 1999. Because access to Russian suppliers was blocked, the compound armour of the T-80UD had to be modified: *Kontakt*-5 ERA blocks and the Ukrainian version (*Varta*) of the Russian *Schtora Soft-Kill System* were applied for further protection.

The T-84 has numerous minor differences and its new, very deep track skirts are striking. It has a thermal imagining unit and laser-rangefinder in the commander's optic. An auxiliary power unit (APU) is installed on the rear track cover right side in an armoured container.

The T-84 *Oplot* (fortress, bastion) has a modified turret with a big overhang at the rear for the automatic loader and ammunition. In the event of an

Type:	T-84
Manufacturer:	KMDB
Battle weight:	46 tonnes
Length:	7085 mm (hull) 9720 mm (with barrel)
Breadth:	3775 mm (with lateral aprons)
Height:	2740 mm (with AA MG)
Motor:	6-cylinder two-stroke 6TD-2 diesel
Efficiency kW/hp:	883/1200
Power/weight ratio:	26.08 hp/tonne
Top speed:	70 km/hr (road)
Fuel capacity:	1300 litres
Range:	540 km
Crew:	3
Armament:	1 x 125 mm KBA3 cannon 1 x 7.62 mm coaxial MG 1 x 12.7 mm AA MG 2 x 6 smoke mortars
Armour:	steel armour, compound and reactive protection
Fording depth:	1.8 m, 5 m with snorkel

The T-84 is a further development of the T-80UD with new, welded turret and Ukrainian components. (KMBD)

The prototype T-84-120 Yatagan is a special export model of the Oplot with a new fire-control installation, 120-mm cannon and automatic loader in the stern. It was offered to Turkey in 2000, but no contract resulted. Bangldesh was also reported to be interested in the Type, but this has not been confiormed. (KMBD)

explosion, the blast pressure escapes through vents in the roof. Around ten *Oplot's* have been taken over so far by the Ukraine. In 2000 under the designation *Yatagan* (Turkish: scimitar) a modified version of the *Oplot* with a 120-mm cannon able to fire NATO ammunition, was offered to Turkey, but no manufacturing contract ensued. The 2008 prototype *Oplot*-M or BM *Oplot* is a substantially modernized variant which bears scarcely any resemblance to a T-80UD. Besides new, modular compound- and reactive *Nosch*-2 armour, this version has improved anti-landmine protection and a new fire-control installation with independent rotatable commander's optics. The tank is compatible for a *Hard-Kill* protective system of the *Zaslon* type.

KMDB is also building on the basis of the T-84 a recovery-tank (BREM-84) and a bridgelayer (MTU-84). Experiments are also being made with an armoured heavy infantry-carrier (BTMP-84).

The T-84 Oplot-M is the newest model of the T-84 family and is fitted with new modular compound- and reactive armour. (KMDB)

M1 Abrams

After the West German-US joint project *Kampfpanzer 70* foundered, in 1971 the United States began the development of a completely new battle tank to replace the already obsolete types M48 and M60. In June 1973 Chrysler (today General Dynamics Land Systems) and General Motors received competitive contracts to build the protoypes, both vehicles being delivered in February 1976. After intensive trials by the US Army the Chrysler model was declared the winner in November 1976. Series production began in 1979 and the first M1 *Abrams* (named for General Creighton Abrams, who had exercised a decisive influence for the development of the Type) was received by the troops in 1980. The M1 was the first Western series-built battle tank to see action equipped with compound armour (*the Chobham* variety developed in Great Britain): it protected the front of the M1 hull and turret. This layered armour was an innovation at that time, gave the tank its typically angular appearance and was substantially more effective against KE and hollow charge missiles than conventional steel armour. The hull sides and bogie (with seven running wheels per side on torsion bar suspension) were protected by heavy track

Type:	M1/M1A
Manufacturer:	General Dynamics Land Systems
Battle weight:	55,700 kg/57 tonnes
Length:	7920 mm (hull) 9770 mm (with barrel)
Breadth:	3657 mm (with lateral aprons)
Height:	2370 mm (upper side turret)
Motor:	Honeywell AGT 1500C gas turbine
Efficiency kW/hp:	1103/1500
Power/weight ratio:	26.93 hp/tonne/26.32 hp/tonne
Top speed:	72 km/hr (road)/ 68 km/hr (road)
Fuel capacity:	1908 litres
Range:	500 km
Crew:	4
Armament:	1 x 120 mm M256 L/44 cannon
	1 x 7.62 mm coaxial MG
	1 x 12.7 mm AA MG and 1 x 7.62 mm AA MG
	2 x 6 smoke mortars
Armour:	steel armour, compound protection
Fording depth:	1.22 m, 1.98 m with preparation

The XM-1 prototype of the Abrams on trials, 1979. (US DoD)

Top: An M1 Abrams waiting to be refuelled during the REFORGER ,84 manouevres, Federal Republic of West Germany, September 1984. (US Army)

Bottom: An early M1 at the Anniston Army Depot, Alabama. (US Army)

guards. The armament of the M1 was originally a 105-mm rifled bore M68 cannon, the US licensed version of the British L7, but the turret was developed from the outset for the 120-mm smooth bore cannon of the *Leopard* 2. The secondary weaponry consisted of a coaxial 7.62-mm MG and a 12.7-mm MG at the commander's hatch, and a 7.62-mm MG at the gunloader's hatch. The ammunition was stored initially in a bunker at the rear of the turret, and isolated from the crew space by armoured doors. The ammunition bunker had blow-out panels overhead for the escape of the blast should the propellant charges detonate. Another novelty of the *Abrams* was its gas-turbine. This unit was very compact and provided high mobility but its high exhaust temperatures created a very distinct IR signature. The greatest drawback of the 1500-hp engine however was its "thirst"; in tests by the Swedish forces in 1993 it was found that the M1 consumed around twice as much fuel as the *Leopard* 2. The turbine and transmission caused problems initially but these were all cured in the course of time.

The arrangement of the crew was conventional (gunlayer and commander right side in the turret, gun loader left side) except that for lack of headroom in the hull the driver was almost in a supine position when his hatch was shut. For night driving he had the benefit of a low light level amplifier. The M1 digital fire-control unit with stabilized optics, laser-rangefinder and crosswind sensor enabled the tank to engage the enemy even when on the move. A thermal imaging unit was available for the detection of targets in poor visibility or darkness. Besides smoke mortars the *Abrams* was also able to make smoke by spraying diesel fuel into the exhaust unit.

From 1984 the turret front armour of the M1 was strengthened and a wire stowage basket fixed around the turret rear, this variant was designated M1 IP (IP=Improved Protection). Many M1 and M1 IP were later upgraded to the A1 version standard being built from August 1985.

The distinguishing characteristic of this version was the 120-mm smooth bore M256 gun (built under West German Rheinmetall L/44 licence). Although the M1A1 looked like the basic model, numerous minor modifications had been made to it, for example a new NBC protection which also served as a heater/air conditioning unit, revised transmission, a 12.7-mm air defence MG which could be aimed and fired from the tank interior, and modified track aprons. The variant M1A1 HA

(HA=Heavy Armour) had the A1 armour reinforced with depleted uranium from 1988, later vehicles of this variant (also known unofficially as HA+) had a thicker uranium layer.

The HA+ version was the basis for the US Marine Corps tank capable of fording deep waters using a snorkel and fitted with improved anti-corrosion protection. From the year 2000 numerous M1A1s were given a thorough overhaul to a practically factory-new state.This enabled the various standards to be assimilated to each other (particularly in upgraded armour) for the installation of new systems such as digitalized communication equipment, an electrical generator (APU) at the rear (to reduce consumption of fuel by the turbine when at rest) and an individual thermal imaging unit for the commander's 12.7-mm MG. These tanks were redesignated M1A1 AIM (AIM=Abrams Integrated Management).

An M1A1HA Abrams of the US Marine Corps, Camp Fallujah, Iraq, January 2007. (USMC)

An M1A1 of the Australian Army leading a group of armoured troop-carrier vehicles Type M113AS4 during a manoeuvre. Puckapunyal Military Area, Australia, May 2010. (Australian Defence Ministry)

M1A2

Construction of the M1A2 began in 1993. It differed from its predecessors primarily for the commander's independent thermal viewer (CITV) which enabled the commander, irrespective of the turret position, to search for targets and notify them to the gunlayer. Furthermore the M1A2 was fitted with a digital battlefield management and information system providing the opportunity to exchange data with similarly equipped vehicles. In order to reduce fuel consumption when the gas-turbine was at rest, an auxiliary electrical generator (APU) is installed at the rear. Previously when the tank came to a standstill the engine had to be kept running to maintain the electrical system. This latter, the fire-control installation, the thermal imaging unit, the ammunition magazine at the rear of the turret and not least the armour have all been improved. The actual production of the M1A2 ended in 1996 but older variants continue to be given general overhauls so that they can be brought up to this standard.

The M1A2 SEP (System Enhancement Programme) includes stronger protection, a new thermal imager for the commander, a new laser-rangefinder and above all a major increase in the efficiency of the on-board computer system. In future the manually operated 12.7-mm MG is to be replaced by a remote weapons station.

Since 2007 several hundred M1s (above all those which were operational in Iraq) have been fitted with a TUSK kit which increases the survivability substantially in built-up areas. This equipment contains amongst other things reactive armour for the track aprons and a wire-cage protection at the rear (later dropped), increased anti-landmine protection, thermal imaging for driver and gun-loader, a protective shield for the gun-loader's MG (which serves partially for the commander's MG), the 12.7-mm MG M2HB on the barrel of the cannon, a powerful searchlight, a TIP (tank infantry phone) enabling support infantry to communicate with the tank crew, and in some cases a rear-view camera. Additionally in the future it is planned to put a remote

Type:	M1A2
Manufacturer:	General Dynamics Land Systems
Battle weight:	63,100 kg
Length:	7920 mm (hull) 9830 mm (with barrel)
Breadth:	3657 mm (with lateral aprons)
Height:	2370 mm (upper side turret) 2885 mm overall)
Motor:	Honetwell AGT 1500C gas turbine
Efficiency kW/hp:	1103/1500
Power/weight ratio:	23.77 hp/tonne
Top speed:	68 km/hr (road)
Fuel capacity:	1908 litres
Range:	425 km
Crew:	4
Armament:	1 x 120 mm M256 L/44 cannon 1 x 7.62 mm coaxial MG 1 x 12.7 mm AA MG and 1 x 7.62 mm AA MG 2 x 6 smoke mortars
Armour:	steel armour, compound protection
Fording depth:	1.22 m, 1.98 m with snorkel

weapons station on the turret roof and a distance-activated protective system.

Since 1991 it has been possible to install an AN/VLQ-6 (later VLQ-8A) *Soft-Kill System* which disrupts the guidance system of incoming anti-tank projectiles. This system was to be located in front of the gun-loader's hatch but on the M1A2 the commander's independent optic already occupied the position.

In the Iraq War of 1991 the M1 proved far superior to the enemy T-55, T-62, T-72 and Type 69s. The thermal imaging units enabled the M1 to make out and destroy its opponents even at night or in conditions of poor visibility at a range of over 2500 metres. Of the approximately 1800 M1s deployed only a few were hit by enemy projectiles, most of which bounced off without effect. Only 23 *Abrams*

An M1A2 of the 3rd Armoured Cavalry Regiment, US Army, in the streets of the town of Tall Afar. The unique recognition characteristic of the M1A2, the commander's independent optic, is in front of the gun-loader's hatch (in the photo to the right). Iraq, 3 February 2005. (US DoD)

Remote weapons station

Loader's Armor Gun Shield

loader's thermal sight

tank/infantry telephone

ermal sight goggles

Rear protecting unit slat armor

Thermal sight components

Abrams Reactive Armore Tiles

This US Army graphic shows the individual components of the TUSK urban kit. The remote MG mount for the turret roof was not installed initially and the MG mount above the cannon is absent from the diagram. (US Army)

reported battle damage, nine sufficiently serious for the tank to be written off. Of these nine, seven were sacrificed to the fire of other M1s and two others reduced to scrap to avoid their falling into enemy hands. Only one M1 crew member fell in action.

During the Iraq War of 2003 the situation was similar. Although the Iraqis succeeded in immobilizing a few M1s, these were then destroyed by their own crews to avoid the capture of the vehicle. No *Abrams* was actually destroyed by enemy fire. On the other hand during the period in Iraq up to 2011 several dozen M1s fell victim to insurgents, principally by improvised explosive devices, and this resulted in a series of crew deaths. The US forces want to retain the M1A1 in active service until at least 2021, and the A2 version beyond the year 2050. At present an A3 variant is being developed but its modifications are down to speculation. The M1A3 would probably have the same or better armour protection but with some decrease in weight and retain elements of the TUSK programme. Besides various experimental vehicles the bridgelayer M104 (*Wolverine* for the Army and *Joint Assault Bridge* for the US Marine Corps), and mine clearance tank M1

A brand-new M1A2 SEP. At the side of the turret are the Abrams Combat Identification Panels which provide a thermal imaging unit with an unmistakable identification. Fort Benning, Georgia, 2012. (US Army)

An M1A2 with TUSK urban kit during operations. The MG mount above the cannon lacks the weapon. Iraq, April 2008. (US Army)

(*Panther II* for the Army, *Assault Breacher Vehicle* for the Marine Corps) were based on the M1. To the time of writing a total of over 9000 M1s of all versions has been built. The US forces use around 5000 at present, and the *Abrams* is also used in Egypt (1005 M1A1, up to 1500 planned), Australia (59 M1A1 AIM), Iraq (140 M1A1 AIM), Kuwait (218 M1A2) and Saudi Arabia (315 M1A2 S9). The export version lacks the depleted uranium armour of the US tanks. The M1 is presently without doubt one of the most powerful and efficient battle tanks in the world. In the last three years up to the time of writing it had taken part in many international competitions for contracts and in general has only been rejected by potential purchasers for its high operational costs (e.g. fuel consumption).